WOMANSPEAK

First published in 1999 by
Marino Books
an imprint of Mercier Press
16 Hume Street Dublin 2
Tel: (01) 661 5299; Fax: (01) 661 8583
E.mail: books@marino.ie

Trade enquiries to CMD Distribution
55A Spruce Avenue
Stillorgan Industrial Park
Blackrock County Dublin
Tel: (01) 294 2556; Fax: (01) 294 2564

© Maeve Conrick 1999

ISBN 1 86023 081 4
10 9 8 7 6 5 4 3 2

A CIP record for this title is available
from the British Library

Cover design by Penhouse Design
Printed in Ireland by ColourBooks,
Baldoyle Industrial Estate, Dublin 13

WOMANSPEAK

MAEVE CONRICK

To Frank and Ian,
the two most wonderful men in my life

ACKNOWLEDGEMENTS

Many people have contributed to the writing of this book. My students and colleagues at University College Cork have provided invaluable assistance by bringing relevant documents to my attention and by commenting on points made in lectures and articles. It is impossible to thank all those whose insights have helped me to formulate my own thoughts on the issues raised in this book.

I would like to thank especially those who read drafts of the manuscript and made very helpful suggestions for improvement: Siobhán McSweeney (New Zealand), Margaret Moriarty (Ottawa), Vera Regan (Dublin) and Margaret Teegan (Cork). Any shortcomings which remain are, of course, attributable only to myself.

I would also like to acknowledge the financial support of the Arts Faculty Research Fund (UCC).

CONTENTS

INTRODUCTION

This book sets out to discuss many varied and controversial issues concerning women and language. Much has been said and written on this subject over many years, but it has become particularly controversial in the last few decades with the resurgence of feminism and the general growth of interest in the status and role of women in society.

Everyone speaks at least one language (except in pathological cases) and all sorts of people have very strong opinions about language. The general public seems particularly interested in matters like 'correctness' and 'standards' of language use. People regularly comment on such topics as pronunciation (especially accent), spelling, grammar and vocabulary. Hardly a day goes by without someone writing to a newspaper editor complaining that a word is not being used with the 'correct' meaning or in the 'correct' context, or that someone has split an infinitive or left a past participle 'dangling'. This is the case especially if the transgression has been committed by a person in the public eye, such as someone working in radio, television or journalism. Such letters usually attract a lot of attention and strength of feeling, with correspondents suggesting, usually with military metaphors, that the English language is under attack and must be vigorously defended if civilisation as we know it is not to disappear without trace, to be replaced by barbarisms of various kinds.

In recent years, the subject matter of letters to editors concerning language has widened to include complaints about innovations regarding the description of women. The issues of sexist and nonsexist language have provoked much comment and debate. Cases in point are the controversies over suggestions by feminists that 'Ms' should replace the traditional 'Miss' and 'Mrs' as the title for women and that forms such as 'chairperson' or 'chairwoman' should replace 'chairman'. The level of heated debate which these two issues alone have generated, and continue to generate, is enormous. Much of the debate rages in the public domain without comment or input percolating through from specialists of language, i.e., linguists. Much of what linguists have to say remains in academic textbooks, Linguistics journals and other formats which are not easily accessible outside the academic context.

My own interest in the subject stems from my twenty years' experience teaching Linguistics in the French Department of University College Cork. During that time, I have lectured and published on various aspects of Linguistics, including Phonetics, Applied Linguistics and Sociolinguistics. Of all the subjects I have broached, the one which has provoked most reaction is the one which constitutes the subject matter of this book – women and language. This field includes discussion of the differences in speech patterns between women and men, and also deals with how women are referred to and described by language.

The principal objective of the book is to bring linguistic insights to bear on the discussion of issues related to the field of women and language – or as the field is more usually entitled 'language and gender' – in a format which is accessible to those who, although not necessarily trained sociolinguists, are interested in what linguists have to say on the linguistic questions raised by the changes in the status and roles of women in modern society. The arguments are based on research carried out in the field of Sociolinguistics, a discipline which investigates and attempts to explain the relationship between language and society.

The two central topics of this book are:
- gender differences in language use
- the portrayal of women and their social roles through language.

The first of these topics concerns how women use language. I will look at the notion of the variation of language in society in general, moving on to address gender-based variation in language. I will look at the background to gender variation and examine stereotypical views of women in society, focusing especially on beliefs about women and their speech patterns.

Chapters 1, 2 and 3 serve as a starting point for an investigation of the various elements of language – pronunciation, grammar and vocabulary – covered in Chapters 4 and 5. The purpose of this analysis is to attempt to answer the age-old question of whether or not women and men 'speak the same language'. The 1990s have seen an enormous growth of interest in the issue of the differences between women's and men's 'conversational styles', and fascinating work has been done on a wide range of issues in the general area of conversational behaviour. Examples of the topics which have received, and continue to receive, most attention include who talks most or takes the longest turns in conversations between mixed groups of women and men, who chooses the topics to be discussed and who interrupts others most frequently. The results of these studies, as will become apparent, do not coincide with the preconceived ideas held by people about what takes place, linguistically speaking, in conversations between women and men.

The second central topic deals – in Chapters 6, 7, 8 and 9 – with the related issue of how women are represented by language. This too has been a controversial area, especially in recent times.

Groups working for change in the status of women propose that language plays a significant role in influencing or even determining how society perceives women. Language has been described as 'sexist,' and attempts have been made to remove sexism from language on the premise that change in language must at least accompany, if not provoke, change in society. Issues such as professional titles for women and the ways in which women are addressed linguistically have become more important with the increased participation of women in the workplace. I will examine – with a linguist's eye – the various recommendations which have been made to promote nonsexist language and the arguments which have been used to resist them.

1

BIMBOS AND BATTLEAXES

STEREOTYPES

Stereotyping is a fact of social life. It involves judging people by reference to characteristics assumed to be shared by groups in society, rather than by reference to individual characteristics or traits. Assigning others to categories is something that people seem to find necessary and reassuring. An obvious category for pigeonholing others is occupation. On social occasions, one of the first questions asked when strangers are introduced is, 'What do you do?' It can be disconcerting for others if you are reluctant to divulge your occupation; people seem to become more relaxed when they can hang some socioeconomic label or other on you.

Not surprisingly, many stereotypes circulate about particular occupations. For whatever reason, lawyer and doctor jokes abound; indeed they often merit whole sections in collections of quotations and witticisms.[1] Inevitably, once you have come clean and told people what you do for a living, unless they share your occupation you are up against all their preconceived ideas of what members of your profession are like. Whatever you say will be interpreted through the prism of conventional wisdom about your chosen occupation and you will have an uphill battle to prove that you are an individual, whose character may not fit into the stereotype. Stereotypes, by their nature, often reduce individuals to one-dimensional caricatures.

NB

GENDER STEREOTYPING

Gender stereotyping is another very pervasive form of stereotyping. General notions of what all women and all men are like are so commonplace as to escape comment when they are trotted out again and again. We regularly hear sentences beginning with, 'Men/women are so . . . ' All areas of human behaviour give rise to stereotypical views and comments: character traits, attitudes, skills, weaknesses. At a very general level, men are commonly believed to be good at mathematical reasoning, ball games, parking, navigation and map-reading, and bad at communication, emotional responsiveness, etc. Women are reputed to be good at languages, communication, emotional sensitivity, precision manual tasks (skills required for activities like sewing and assembling electronic circuit boards) and bad at mathematical reasoning and spatial skills. Women's 'failings', especially their supposed lack of prowess with parking cars, are often the subject of jokes. The following remark made by actor and film director Woody Allen aptly reflects the stereotypical view:

From where she parked the car it was a short walk to the footpath.[2]

Categorising people according to preconceived ideas about gender attributes has little, if any, value and may have detrimental results if children are steered in a particular direction as a result of notions about what is appropriate for girls or boys. Not all boys shine at mathematics, nor do all girls perform well at languages, yet in the past the established pattern in schools was to teach the more 'manly' scientific subjects like Physics, Chemistry, Mathematics and Technical Graphics to boys and teach Languages and 'practical' subjects like Home Economics to girls. When I was in secondary school, in Ireland in the 1960s, it was the era of 'Girls don't do honours [higher level]', especially not in Mathematics. Who knows how many budding female mathematicians were frustrated and how many boys did not get the opportunity to learn several modern languages as a result of these biased assumptions? In the more enlightened 1990s, greater efforts are made to encourage girls and boys to consider non-traditional subjects and, consequently, careers. Although times have certainly changed a lot, many of the old attitudes still prevail and are perpetuated in subject choices available for boys and girls in second-level education. The distribution of subjects taught by male and female teachers tends also to follow traditional patterns, in that Home Economics is usually taught by women and Woodwork and Metalwork by men.

In recent years, society has become more conscious of

the images of women and men that are being projected – often unwittingly – in educational materials. Studies have been carried out on gender bias in school textbooks, and recommendations for a more equitable gender distribution and depiction of gender roles have been made to those responsible for the preparation and implementation of curricula. Examples include the British Council/ELT's *Guidelines for the Representation Of Women And Men*, and the Irish National Teachers Organisation's (INTO) *Fair Play for Girls and Boys in Primary Schools*. Guidelines on avoiding gender stereotyping refer to how pervasive the practice is. The objective they hope to achieve is to make people – especially those in positions of influence, like teachers and writers of school textbooks – rethink the gender stereotyping they may, unconsciously, be perpetuating. There are many examples of schools using gender re-education material, teaching modules on English and Gender which try to raise consciousness about gender stereotyping as encountered in stories for children. One example is *Fairy Stories and Folk Tales*, compiled and written by Bronwyn Mellor with Judith Hemming and Jane Leggett. The authors explain why they chose to base the textbook on these materials with the following comment:

> stories are one of the ways by which we are taught about the world we live in and how we are expected to behave in it as girls and boys, men and women.[3]

Recognising Gender Stereotyping

Gender stereotyping may apply to many aspects of human behaviour, including:

Physical Appearance

- Appearance is regarded as more significant for women, who tend to be described by reference to physical attributes (e.g., 'a leggy blonde') or dress, where such a description would be unlikely for men. (e.g., 'The blonde new committee member arrived at the meeting, dressed in a fetching blue suit.')

- Women's appearance attracts more comment than men's. It is more common to hear women being told something like, 'You are looking particularly attractive today' or 'Blue really suits you'. Alluding to a man's appearance is more unusual and such comments are likely to be considered too personal.

Character Traits

- Men may be portrayed as strong, logical, capable, assertive.

- Women, conversely, may be portrayed as emotional, uncertain, vulnerable, in need of protection, and even weak and inept.

Social Roles

- Women may still be considered primarily or exclusively as homemakers.

- Women may be identified in relation to their domestic relationships rather than as individuals in their own right. (e.g., 'Mary Jones, wife of the well-known businessman John Jones, has accepted an offer to work with a major company.')

Occupational Roles

- Some occupations are considered to be more typically male or female. Women are generally regarded as more suited to the 'caring professions' such as nursing, teaching and social work, while occupations such as fire-fighting or train driving are considered to be 'men's work'.

The physical strength that many jobs required in the past is no longer necessary, however, because advances in technology have brought more automation. A rail company employee is quoted as saying, in reference to train driving, 'In the old days, there was a lot of heavy lifting, but it's all hi-tech now, so it's easier for women and wee men.'[4] Moreover, professions dominated by women are not necessarily easy or light in terms of the physical strength required. Nursing, for example, involves a lot of strenuous work such as lifting patients. So the old stereotypes about what is 'men's work' and 'women's work' – even if they were based on requirements of physical strength in the past – no longer hold true.

In many cases, the existing gender stereotypes may have very little to do with the lives of modern women. In most Western societies, an increasing number of women work outside the home; many women are the sole breadwinner, bringing up children in one-parent families. The United Nations data published in *The World's Women 1995: Trends and Statistics* describe the increased economic participation of women worldwide as follows:

Over the past two decades, women's reported economic activity rates increased in all regions except sub-Saharan Africa and eastern Asia, and all of these increases are large except in eastern Europe, central Asia and Oceania. In fact, women's labour force participation increased more in the 1980s than in the 1970s in many regions. In contrast, men's economic activity rates have declined everywhere except central Asia.[5]

This trend is apparent in Ireland too as women are entering the workforce twice as fast as men, according to the most recent Census in 1996. Figures published in 1998 show that there was an increase of about 150,000 in the workforce, made up of 49,000 men and 102,000 women.[6] Irish women now make up 42 per cent of the workforce, as opposed to only 28.2 per cent in the early 1970s, so the change is very significant. In the business sector, 20 per cent of all registered businesses are owned by women and, in 1997 40 per cent of all new businesses registered were started up by women.[7] Consequently, it does not make sense to continue to portray women only in traditional roles like housekeepers or as being in need of protection.

The Proverbial Woman
A rich source of information on stereotypical attitudes to women is provided by proverbs, which contain much conventional wisdom gathered over centuries. The *Oxford Dictionary of English Proverbs* (Wilson, 1970) contains 106 proverbs that include the words 'woman/women'. Of

these references, only about thirteen have anything positive or affirming to say about women! The picture that emerges makes depressing reading. Women are proverbially labelled as changeable, weak, noisy, vain, deceptive, foolish, mischievous ... Here are some typical examples:

> *Woman is the confusion (woe) of man.*
> *A woman is the weaker vessel.*
> *Woman's mind and winter wind change oft.*
> *Tell a woman she is fair and she will soon turn fool.*
> *Where there are women and geese, there wants no noise.*
> *Women (wives and wind) are necessary evils.*
> *Women are the devil's nets.*
> *Women naturally deceive, weep and spin.*

Most of these proverbs are now obsolete, but they do encapsulate some very common attitudes which have persisted. Of the ten specific references made to women in the more recent *Concise Oxford Dictionary of Proverbs* (Simpson, 1982)[8], it is difficult to find a complimentary one. Some are ambiguous. One well-known proverb, still in current usage, suggests that *'A woman's work is never done.'* Is it saying that women are hard-working, or that they should never stop working? Given the negative portrayal of women in proverbs, as evidenced above, it is difficult to take the first interpretation as the more likely.

Among the other proverbs included in that volume are the following, equally uncomplimentary, examples:

A man is as old as he feels, a woman as old as she looks.

Silence is a woman's best garment.

Six hours sleep for a man, seven for a woman, and eight for a fool.

Another *Dictionary of Proverbs*, compiled by Rosalind Fergusson in 1983, tells the same sorry tale. This text contains 104 entries under the main heading *'Women'* and this is further divided into subheadings according to common themes. The subheadings themselves speak volumes about the general tenor of the perception of women which the proverbs illustrate:

Women:

Their danger

Their value

Their capriciousness

Their impulsiveness

Their wilfulness

Their dissimulation

Their tears

Their lack of wisdom

Their reasoning

Their tongue

Their needs

Their duties

Handling women

Man and woman

It would be interesting to consider whether men are portrayed, proverbially, in an equally unflattering way. However, it is impossible to compare the treatment of women and men since many proverbs contain references to 'man' or 'men', as generic, i.e., referring to all human beings rather than male human beings only. Sometimes it is difficult to know which use is intended, so any comparison is inconclusive. (See Chapter 7 on the use of 'man')

WOMEN IN QUOTATIONS

Another rich source of material on attitudes to women is provided by books containing collections of quotations. In 1993, the editors of *New Woman* published a collection of quotations that appeared in the magazine between 1983 and 1993 with the title *Sounds Like a New Woman,* which exemplified attitudes to women, held by both men and women – mostly well-known public figures in the United States. The quotations are divided into two categories, those which 'sound like a new woman' and those which deserve a 'thump on the head' for displaying sexist attitudes.

The 'thump' pages provide plenty of quotations to confirm that traditional stereotypes about women and how they behave – or should behave – have not died with obsolete proverbs but, even towards the end of the twentieth century, are alive and well. The quotations selected in the 'thump' section of the text characterise women as dumb, changeable, confused, helpless, in need of a man's protection and only good at cooking, cleaning and looking after children. The authors suggest that the recommendations about women's behaviour which emanate from the 'thump' pages, suggest ' . . . how they should stay out of male-dominated professions (like sports, sports refereeing, and politics, to name a few), how they should keep their mouths shut and their men happy in bed.'[9]

The belief that if women are at all physically attractive, they must be 'bimbos' is not a figment of a malicious imagination. A test pilot is reported to have begun a talk on supersonic flight with the warning to women that 'Some of the better-looking ones here won't understand what I'll be talking about.'[10] If it was a joke it was in very bad taste. The possibility of someone finding such a 'joke' funny says something about the kind of society we live in, if it permits or encourages the targeting of groups of women in such a demeaning way. Much irony is apparent too in the fact that Western society places such value on women's appearance. It seems that women cannot win: if they do not give in to the prevailing ethos in the pursuit of feminine beauty they are unattractive and unfeminine, but if they do cultivate their appearance they run the risk of being considered bimbos.

In the book *Sounds Like a New Woman*, references to women's appearance are frequent. In the USA, a State Board of Education member made this comment, in 1991, to Ann Richards, Governor of Texas:

> I think you're the prettiest governor I've ever talked to.

Her reply was:

> I hope one day you'll think I'm the smartest governor you've ever talked to![11]

It is difficult to imagine such a comment being addressed to a man in a comparable situation. It appears that women, even in very senior professional positions, still have to put up with their appearance being considered an appropriate subject for comment.

THE WORKING WOMAN

Since there are more and more women in the workplace, occupying a greater number and variety of positions, gender expectations at work have become a subject of discussion. Many of the stereotypes about women's character and behaviour in the wider world have been carried over to the world of work. Colleagues may be very quickly disabused of the stereotypical notions that women are 'feminine', gentle, and behave like ladies at all times when they are faced with a confident, capable and strong-willed female boss. Because confidence, capability and strong will are expected from men but not from women, if women show any signs of strength of will or (perish the thought!) ruthlessness, they are viewed more negatively than men who display similar behavioural characteristics. As Gloria Steinem, founding editor of *Ms.* magazine, puts it:

> A man can be called ruthless if he bombs a country into oblivion. A woman can be called ruthless if she puts you on hold.[12]

Even when men and women use the same styles of behaviour, they may be interpreted very differently. A woman who exhibits a strong style is likely to be considered a battleaxe, whereas a man may just be considered efficient at getting things done. Even in advertising, on the rare occasions when women are portrayed as holding executive positions, they are often described as battle-axes. A scenario from the current television advertising campaign for Kenco coffee provides a typical example. The episode involves a female secretary, who is about to begin work for a new female boss, meeting another woman in the lift and referring to her new boss's repu-tation for being a battleaxe. The twist in the story is – to the dismay of the secretary – that the woman in the lift turns out to be the boss herself, who, luckily, takes the criticism in good part.

Ambition may be highly regarded in a man but frowned on as 'too pushy', 'unladylike' and therefore 'not nice' in a woman. The following list exemplifies some of the possi-bilities for differences in interpretation:

A man is assertive, a woman is aggressive.

A man is firm, a woman is stubborn.

A man is attentive to detail, a woman is picky.

A man says what he thinks, a woman is opinion-ated.

A man exercises authority, a woman is tyrannical.

A man is discreet, a woman is secretive.

A man has high standards, a woman is difficult to work for.

The questions raised by these different gender-based interpretations go far beyond reaction to instances of individual behaviour. They challenge the deeply held –

often unconscious – beliefs held by people about the innate differences between men and women.

THE TALKATIVE WOMAN

As well as commonsense beliefs and stereotypes about women's behaviour in general, there are many stereotypical views of women's language and communicative skills. Women, it is thought, use fewer taboo words like swear words and are more polite, more conservative and less assertive than men in their speech patterns. Probably the most enduring stereotype about women's speech is that they talk a lot, usually about trivial subjects, and that they make a lot of noise. That women's speech is regarded as synonymous with noise is evident in a commonly used metaphor that describes a group of women talking as being like 'a gaggle of geese', and the belief that women talk a lot is summed up in the phrase 'Telephone, telegramme, tell-a-woman'.

The dictionaries of proverbs to which I referred above (Wilson 1970, Simpson 1982 and Fergusson 1983) are rich in examples which suggest that women are archetypal high achievers when it comes to talking and, furthermore, that it would be salutary for them to cultivate silence. The following are representative examples:

Woman's tongue is the last thing about her that dies.
Woman's tongue wags like a lamb's tail
Women are great talkers.
Women will have the last word.
Women will say anything.

Where there are women and geese there wants no noise.
Silence is the best ornament of a woman.
Silence is a woman's best garment.
A woman's sword is her tongue and she does not let it rust.
A sieve will hold water better than a woman's mouth a secret.
Maidens must be mild and meek, swift to hear and slow to speak. [13]

The English-speaking world is not alone in its assumption that women are 'chatterboxes'. Exactly the same views are expressed by proverbs in French – and they are probably shared by many other linguistic groups too.

Où femme y a, silence n'y a.
(Where there is a woman, there is no silence.)
Il y a mille inventions pour faire parler les femmes, mais pas une pour les faire taire.
(There are thousands of ways of making women talk, but not one to make them stop.)

Irish too has its share of proverbs commenting on the verbosity of women.

An áit m-biann mná biann caint, a's an áit a m-biann géidh biann callán.
(Wherever there are women there is talking; and wherever there are geese there is cackling.)

> *Trí nithe ná tagann meirg ortha, – teanga mná,*
> *crúite capaill búistéara, airgead lucht carthannachta.*
> (Three things that never rust – a woman's tongue,
> the shoes of a butcher's horse, charitable folk's
> money.)[14]

It seems that the supposed verbosity of women (and
men's efforts to keep them quiet!) are represented in
proverbs internationally. There are plenty of modern
examples too. Pieter Botha, when he was President of
South Africa, is reported to have replied to a female
heckler in 1986:

> 'Be quiet! Didn't your husband teach you not to
> interrupt when a man is talking?'[15]

An even more recent example can be gleaned from a book
by Ken Carlton, called *Date Talk, Dinner Talk, Pillow Talk*
(1998), which leaves us under no illusion about what the
author thinks is the best conversational strategy for
women:

> The greatest conversation I've ever had with a
> woman consisted mainly of silence.[16]

With such a collection of precepts for women to follow,
it is hardly surprising that when girls are being taught
to 'behave like ladies', part of the training is not to speak
much, and certainly not to interrupt men.

Gossip

As well as being considered (overly) talkative, the subject matter of women's talk is often regarded as trivial. Much of what women discuss is relegated to the realm of gossip, or idle chatter. The aphorism 'men talk, women gossip' expresses this stereotype very succinctly. To realise that 'gossip' is usually used pejoratively, and chiefly to refer to women, one only has to consult *The Shorter Oxford English Dictionary,* which defines 'a gossip' as: 'a person, mostly a woman, who delights in idle talk; a tattler.' The verb 'to gossip' is defined as: 'to talk idly, mostly about other people's affairs; to go about tattling.' The word 'gossip' originally meant a sponsor at a baptism (either male or female) but, by the mid sixteenth century, its meaning had degenerated to the meaning given above and it had become more specialised in referring to women. Nowadays, it has become so identified with women that any man so described would see it as an affront to his masculinity. He might even be called 'an old woman', which would be the height of ridicule for a man!

The negative associations of 'gossip' have been challenged, not only by feminists but also by psychologist Robin Dunbar, who sees gossip as playing an important social and evolutionary function. In his book *Grooming, Gossip and the Evolution of Language* (1996), Dunbar suggests that gossip played (and continues to play) an essential role in social cohesion, as a form of 'mutual grooming'. Far from perceiving gossip as a waste of time, he puts forward the idea that language evolved not to allow men in primitive societies to plan their hunting activities better, but to allow women to gossip. It is a very interesting theory, which rehabilitates gossip and attributes greater importance than is conventionally attributed to women in the evolutionary stakes, at least with regard to linguistic development.

The linguist Deborah Tannen, in her book *You Just Don't Understand: Women and Men in Conversation* (1992), takes a slightly different angle on the issue by suggesting that the negative connotations of 'gossip' come from the fact that it is part of oral rather than written language. In her view, when something is written down rather than dealt with orally, society accords it more significance and value – whatever the subject matter:

> When people talk about the details of daily lives, it is gossip; when they write about them it is literature: short stories and novels.[17]

One cannot help but think that the novels of a writer like Jane Austen, which describe a very circumscribed world, could very well, in an oral context, be dismissed as gossip.

When men get together, it is considered normal for them to discuss topics like their work, sport or politics, rather than their families or homes, which are belittled as 'women's topics'. It could also be argued that when women who do not work outside the home talk about their families and homes and the details of their daily lives, they are, in fact, talking about the same subject as men, i.e., their work. The only problem is that their work within the home is not highly regarded – it may not even be considered to merit the name 'work' at all – so any discussion of it is seen as relatively unimportant in comparison to men's discussion of 'real' work. In that sense, it is not the relative or comparative value of the work itself which is in question, but simply the fact that work which primarily women are engaged in has less value attributed to it.

The difference in value attributed to activities – and in the kind of language used to describe them – depending on whether they are accomplished by women or men – is evident in the findings from a study of a village in New Foundland, carried out by James Farris in 1963. It revealed that when women assembled, their talk was referred to as 'gossip', whereas when men gathered in a similar way at a trading post, their conversations were described as an exchange of 'news'.[18]

WHAT ARE THEY TALKING ABOUT?

The topics discussed by women are generally considered to be trivial because they focus primarily on the private sphere of the home, rather than on the 'more important' public sphere of politics or the marketplace. Most men tend to find discussions of such topics as choosing home decor, sewing or cooking (the daily kind rather than the gourmet kind) intensely boring, while women may find interminable discussions of cars, golf or football games equally tedious. It is difficult to say that one set of topics is, objectively, more significant or essential than the other. It all depends on your point of view and which activity is important to you. At one level, it is laughable to think of twenty-two grown men running around a football field after a soccer ball. In another context, rugby players heavily involved in a scrummage make an equally

– if not more – hilarious picture. But, for some people, mainly men, soccer and rugby are akin to a religion. For some women, matching the carpet and the curtains in the living room may be of crucial importance and entail numerous visits to home decor and furniture shops. Who is to say which activity is objectively more important or interesting? There is no answer, other than to say that for each of us some things are important and other things leave us indifferent. Each individual or group may fail to appreciate the importance of the other's interests.

The result may be that communication and understanding between men and women is often considered to be so difficult that they seem to be speaking 'different languages'. This is obviously an exaggeration, but the stereotype that men find women impossible to understand – and that this failure of communication has something to do with language – is so commonplace as to be a cliché. Denis Boyles, in his (very) tongue-in-cheek *The Modern Man's Guide to Modern Women* (1993), puts it like this:

> There are two distinct language families from which all modern Western tongues are descended. One is Indo-European. The other is girl-talk ... Girl-talk is a difficult tongue to master. Women ... are speak–ing a language so obscure that not even other women can always be sure of what they're talking about. Hence, "What do you mean by that?" is the reply given by most women to almost anything said by almost anyone.[19]

The main explanation behind the notion that it is impossible for men to understand women is that women do not 'say what they mean', or at least not in the direct way that men are reputed to use. And so, women are described as incomprehensible and devious. Many books have been written and fortunes made 'explaining' what women 'really mean', but, if we believe much of what is written about communication between the sexes, the answer to Freud's now proverbial question 'What do women want?' is still shrouded in mystery.

CONCLUSION

The picture that emerges from many sources of how women behave, or are supposed to behave, is not a very complimentary one. Despite the big changes in women's roles and contributions to society in recent decades, many of the clichés about women – that they are either bimbos or battleaxes – and their capabilities (or lack of them) still persist. Many girls are still being encouraged (however subtly) to pay a lot of attention to their appearance and to become 'ladies'. Despite the great advances that have come about up to the late 1990s, working women are still not reaching the heights of achievement in their chosen professions, or at least not in the same numbers as men. The novelty of women bosses means that there are not yet enough women in place for a distinctive style to emerge, and judgements of women in high places are often based on stereotypical views of what is appropriately 'feminine' behaviour. Society's expectations of how women should behave indicate that what is considered appropriate is still circumscribed by very traditional, often erroneous ideas about the nature of women and their talents.

Language and women's use of it, along with many other factors, play a part in forming the impression that society has of women. It is still believed that women are prolific talkers and that they spend most of their time chattering and gossiping about unimportant things. In some of the following chapters we will consider these and other stereotypes about women's speech patterns and compare them with objective research carried out to ascertain whether or not they have any basis in reality.

2

GENDER IN THE MEDIA AND ADVERTISING

GENDER IN THE MEDIA

Probably the most striking examples of gender stereo-typing are evident in the media, especially in the visual images on television and in magazines and newspapers. The portrayal of gender roles – as well as gender attributes – gives rise to much comment and criticism, especially from feminists, who are conscious of how such treatment reinforces limited views of women and their roles and capabilities.

Even more significant is the lack of adequate representation of women in coverage of events from sports to politics. The lack of reporting on women's sporting events, or their relegation to less popular slots on television or radio, sends a clear message that their status is secondary, and that men's events are more important. The women's tennis singles final at Wimbledon takes place on the second-last day and the men's singles final on the last day, as the latter is the highlight of the whole competition. This order of things has, until recently, gone largely unquestioned – things have always been done this way and no one seems to consider challenging the status quo or its rationale, which, presumably, is associated with money and sponsorship. In Ireland in recent years circumstances have obliged journalists to cover women's sporting events, since Irish women, more than Irish men, have been hitting the heights in international competitions. The achievements of Irish athletes like Sonia O'Sullivan and Catherina McKiernan have ensured front-page coverage for women's events.

When reference is made by the media to 'expert opinion,' it is regularly assumed to be male, especially in 'important' subject areas like economics, politics or international relations. Women may be called in as experts only in areas that are regarded as 'women's issues', such as parenting, abortion and contraception, as if only these areas were relevant to women's lives, (and as if they were only relevant to women's lives). This tendency has supported women's continued exclusion from the public domain, relegating them to the private domain and thus perpetuating the 'separate domain' ideology that has locked both women and men into constricting moulds. Maurine H. Beasley (1997) describes the situation as it pertains to women in the USA (although her comments are relevant worldwide) as follows:

> ... women are now given limited credibility in the public arena. Female experts may appear in the news when the topic is abortion or affirmative action, but 'when the topic is war, foreign policy, the environment, or national purpose, female voices, and feminist voices, in particular, are ignored' ... Women

still are not full participants in the democratic political process.[20]

Some of the more prevalent images of women in the media fit into the category of 'decoration'. Photos of presentations of trophies and prizes regularly depict women who do not appear to have any connection with the event being recorded, and seem to have no function other than to look pretty. Consequently, the women sometimes remain nameless, since their purpose is purely to add visual attractiveness. This portrayal of women is similar to their use in car advertising as decorative objects draped over the vehicles.

GENDER IN ADVERTISING

Advertising reflects and, to some extent, may help to define the social roles of women and men. In the case of the portrayal of women, there appears to be something of a time lag. The point is often made that although the roles of women in society have changed dramatically over the last thirty years, women are still portrayed primarily as homemakers or as sex objects by the advertising industry. Guy Cook in *The Discourse of Advertising* (1992) suggests that, although advertisements for cars are no longer exclusively directed at men, those that include women in their target group still portray them in a more limited series of roles than they portray men:

While perfume ads appeal to both men and women almost exclusively as lovers, there is a difference in the presentation of the two sexes in car ads. Men are not only lovers but also husbands, fathers, loners, careerists, technical experts, general status-seekers and responsible guardians of the planet's ecology(!); women are almost always only wives, lovers or careerists. [21]

When women are used as sex objects in advertising, they are displayed as scantily clad and provocative, being used to promote any product imaginable. Advertisements for cars seem to be particularly popular for displaying decorative women. For example, the current advertising campaign for the Citroën Xsara uses a scantily clad Claudia Schiffer in television and magazine advertisements in both English and French. Maybe this is connected with the idea, in some people's minds, that cars and other inanimate objects are somehow – despite not having gender – female. 'How is she going for you?' is, for some, a way of enquiring about the mechanical condition of someone's car.

Expanses of female flesh are a regular feature of certain types of newspapers. Women's bodies – especially legs – are reduced to body parts in advertisements, a process which objectifies the person, by not representing them as complete people. While images of women's legs are at least relevant when advertising women's tights, pictures of women's legs or parts of legs are not at all necessary or appropriate in the many other circumstances in which they are used. An advertisement for the Kerry-gold Horseshow in Dublin in the summer of 1998 is conspicuous by the absence of pictures of horses (except in the logo). Instead, the advertisement is dominated by a large colour photo of a woman's legs, from hips to heels, with short skirt and high heels, accompanied by the caption 'The Height of Summer'.[22] One wonders what inference is being drawn. Could there possibly be an association between women and horseflesh?! The association of ideas is made even more explicit when a woman is described as 'a fine filly'.[23]

In the context of the portrayal of women in the traditional role of homemaker, several classic advertisements spring to mind. One of the enduring images produced by advertisers on television is the mother in the Oxo advertisement who waits on the family at table, solves all interpersonal conflict, and keeps everyone happy with delicious gravy. Another one is the Shake'n'Vac housewife dancing happily around the house vacuuming to her heart's content – or so the promoters would have us believe! Some advertisements for baby-food and baby-wear are still exclusively aimed at mothers, although it seems hardly credible nowadays – or even in the past – that only mothers buy clothes and food for their babies. A Heinz/Farley's advertisement reassured its customers (only mothers?) in 1996 that:

Mothers can continue to choose our baby foods with complete confidence . . . [24]

It is, to some extent at least, understandable that advertisers of products traditionally associated with women's and, more particularly, mothers' roles direct their attention primarily to women, but one would not expect it to continue to be directed exclusively to them. There is incontrovertible proof that the social reality of women's and men's roles continues to change. The number of house-husbands in Britain has more than doubled from 44,000 in 1992 to 98,000 in 1996.[25] So, the evidence is there that men working in the home are a growing market, not to mention the increasing number of men who share child-rearing duties with partners who work outside the home. Promoters are foolish to ignore these changes in the composition of their target groups. In the example discussed above, it would have been so easy – and un-controversial – to include all categories by using 'parents' rather than 'mothers'. Pampers now uses a television advertisement which describes its product inclusively as 'the favourite nappy with mums, dads and babies.'

Despite these documented changes, even advertise-ments for technologically advanced products fall back on very conventional stereotypes of women's roles. It is surprising to see modern organisations like computer companies, which are (in theory at least) at the cutting edge of social progress, continuing to use advertisements which give a very limited picture of women's roles, trotting out yet again the jaded stereotypes of decades ago. A recent example of a recruitment advertisement from Dell computers, apparently aimed at 'trendy' young people (telling them not to bother about dressing up for interview, as 'being the best at what you do' is the most important requirement) has the caption:

Tell your mother to put the iron away and just come as you are.[26]

This might not seem so depressing if there were many other advertisements portraying women in a wide variety of careers and roles, although, on a more positive note, the Disney company, at the same time as updating Mickey Mouse's image, has also updated Minnie Mouse's. While she was confined to the home in earlier cartoons, she has now become a 'self-confident professional, working as one of the world's only female conductors of an international orchestra'![27]

There is evidence that girls are subjected to pressure from magazines aimed specifically at teenagers to do little else other than look good and get a boyfriend. A recent study of a selection of these publications shows that advertising in their pages is devoted substantially to products associated with appearance, such as cosmetics and clothes.[28] The message that 'getting a man' is an essential objective for teenage girls is clear and some-times made explicit. One advertisement got directly to the point:

Forget agony aunts, problem pages and your best friend. We'll work day and night to get you a man.

Reading these words can make you wonder if you are living in a time warp, where reality has not changed for at least a generation.

Admittedly, it is not obligatory to buy magazines, nor is it compulsory to look at advertising on television, but it has become impossible to live in the modern world without being assailed on all fronts by some form of advertising, probably the most pervasive being billboards, which are unavoidable if you – as most people do – use the public roads. Unlike journalists, advertisers do not have a moral obligation to portray society accurately. Their only objective is to sell their clients' products; they do not have to consider the impressions they are conveying and the stereotypes they are reinforcing. The brief of watchdog organisations monitoring the advertising industry, such as the Advertising Standards Authorities, is to ensure that certain standards of consumer protection are adhered to and that public decency is not offended, but their agenda does not include attempting to combat stereotyping. One cannot blame advertising agencies for doing their job, but it is an unfortunate reality that their influence, especially on the impressionable young, is powerful, and in many cases their portrayal of the modern woman is limited and misleading.

A very blatant form of gender stereotyping in advertising is evident in how regularly the authoritative male voice-over is featured. How often do we see helpless women toiling trying to make their washing whiter than white and having this terrible problem solved by a self-assured male voice telling them their worries are over if they use brand X washing powder? Guy Cook, in *The Discourse of Advertising*, describes it as follows:

> Perhaps the most telling evidence of sexism in advertising is not to be found in 'what happens', but in the ubiquity of the male in the voice-over, even in ads portraying or aimed at women, or which pay lip-service to the modern 'liberated woman'![29]

Even in that most traditional role of housekeeping – keeping the family's washing up to standard – women are portrayed as lacking in competence, needing the help of a man to get it right.

The advertising industry also makes use of the reputation that women have for talking a lot, especially in the case of clients such as telecommunications companies who make their money from the amount of time people talk on the telephone. A notable example is the British Telecom advertising campaign called 'It's good to talk'. In 1994, British Telecom ran a newspaper advertising campaign, the point of which was to encourage men to behave 'like women', i.e., to talk more on the telephone. The text of the advertisement was a revealing illustration of the differences between men's and women's communicative styles.

Why can't men be more like women ?
Women and men communicate differently.
Have you noticed?
Women like to sit down to make phone calls.
They know that getting in touch is more important than what you actually say.
Men adopt another position.
They stand up.
Their body language says this message will be short, sharp and to the point. 'Meet you down the pub, all right? See you there.'
That's a man's call.
Women can't understand why men are so abrupt.

The message that women talk about trivial matters is abundantly clear, since 'they know that getting in touch is more important than what you actually say'. If men's message is 'to the point', when being contrasted with women's, then what the latter have to say deals with irrelevancies. Another interesting aspect of this particular advertisement is the fact that the man and woman in the illustration are wearing no clothes (although the caption is strategically placed in order to spare readers' blushes). One assumes that the suggestion being made is that there is something 'natural', and therefore biologically determined, about the linguistic behavioural patterns of women and men, as described in the advertisement. This is a very controversial insinuation.

CONCLUSION

Whether in proverbs, in the media or in advertising, the representation of women is often false and limited and leaves a lot to be desired. Despite the huge social changes of recent decades, it seems that many of the old attitudes linger on and are perpetuated in a wide spectrum of contexts. Gender stereotypes are deeply ingrained and persist even when reality shows them to be no longer – if they were ever – relevant. What is most alarming is that many people do not even realise that they are disadvantaging women by categorising them in very limited ways. There are a number of consequences for women resulting from these often unconscious attitudes. The 'glass ceiling' is difficult to explain in societies which do not actively discriminate against the employment and promotion of women in the workplace. A partial explanation may lie in the prevalence of attitudes towards women which, because they are unconscious, are not usually the subject of overt discussion. If negative and limited images of women are prevalent in the media and elsewhere – in other words, if their portrayal falls into a limited number of categories – it seems obvious that such typecasting plays a role in the construction and maintenance of prevailing opinion about the abilities and aptitudes of women.

There is evidence that the public is becoming more aware and more discerning about the representation of women in advertising. The Advertising Standards Authority in Britain is quoted, in August 1998, as stating that the public is becoming increasingly concerned about the use of sexism, among other things, in advertisements.[30] The bottom line for commercial enterprises is that, if sexist advertising has a negative effect on business, advertisers will have to change their approach.

3

VARIETY IS THE SPICE OF LANGUAGE

VARIATION

Of all the things that are said about language, one statement can be made with conviction: language varies a lot. This statement might seem like a cliché, so obvious that everyone knows it to be true. Nonetheless, many people behave as if language is unchanging, an immutable object. In many people's minds there is 'The English Language', or 'The French Language', rather than several forms and varieties of English or French as the case may be. This is partly because our view of the nature of language is based on our experience of European languages like English, French, Spanish, Italian and German, which have a long history of being committed to writing. In fact, when people are requested to give examples of 'good' or 'correct' English, they usually provide examples from a written source, especially from writers of 'great' literature. The conviction that a language is encapsulated in one form of that language, usually the written form, fosters the opinion that no one should ever attempt to change this unique object of reverence which is 'The English Language'.

Since the written form of a language changes more slowly than the spoken form, speakers of languages with a strong written tradition may be under the impression that the language they speak is more static than it is in reality. Spoken English, for example, has changed much more significantly than written English over the last few centuries, although this is not immediately apparent since the written language has not adapted to take account of changes in oral grammar. Even in a relatively short time, such as a generation, changes in spoken English are noticeable. The BBC Television broadcast from Alexandra Palace on 31 August 1936 is often replayed as it is an important historical document; it was the first time a female television announcer made an appearance on BBC television. In the 1990s, it is obvious to all that even those British people who speak with what is called a 'Received Pronunciation' (RP) accent no longer speak with the rather stilted accent used by the announcer in that broadcast[31], but written English has not shown a corresponding level of change since that time.

Variation, particularly in spoken language, is a reality in the situation of any linguistic group, and may be manifested over time as mentioned above, or at a given point in time. The extent to which language varies from one context to another at a given point in time is probably not widely understood or appreciated. Social class accents, i.e., patterns of pronunciation based on differences in socio-economic grouping, represent probably the best-known example of variation. Language varies on all levels between individuals belonging to different social groups – at the level of pronunciation as well as in terms of vocabulary and grammar – and such differences (usually called inter-speaker variation) on all levels of language are referred to as 'social dialects'.[32] What is less widely appreciated is the amount of variation in the speech of an individual (often called intra-speaker variation) depending on the social context he or she happens to be in. People adjust their speech to the context they find themselves in, whether it is talking on the telephone, giving an interview or chairing a meeting. As a rule, people will adopt more prestigious forms of accent or dialect if they feel they are being evaluated. Linguists call this 'style-shifting'.

Some of the most important factors which affect language use are:

- Socio-economic class – a difficult to define category which can include such factors as parental and family background, education and profession
- Regional differences – based on geographical factors, including place of birth (region and country) and subsequent linguistic contact, and place of residence
- Age – older people will not share the same vocabulary, for example, as younger people
- Gender – an obvious difference between male and female is the difference in pitch, higher for women than for men
- Social context – individuals speak more formally in situations like meetings and less formally when conversing with their friends

The fact that there is an interplay between all the different factors adds another dimension of complexity to the reality of variation. For example, regional accents are affected by socio-economic class: not everyone from the same geographical area speaks with exactly the same accent. People who change their accent – by moving geographically or socially – may revert to using features of their original accent when they meet family and friends. The result of this large-scale variation is the rich pattern of differentiation which characterises all languages and their speakers. The wealth of data available provides plenty of opportunities for research and discussion.

SEX AND GENDER

It was not fully appreciated until recent years, particularly with the influence of the women's movement in the 1970s and the increase in interest in Sociolinguistics, that gender is a very significant source of variation in language. Differences in language based on sex seem obvious. Everyone knows, for example, that the voice quality of men and women is not the same, and one can identify with almost one hundred per cent accuracy whether someone speaking on the telephone is male or female. Men generally use lower pitch, i.e., have lower voices, than women, and this lower tone results from the physiological fact that men generally have a larger larynx than women.[33] What became obvious as researchers began to study the speech of women and men more extensively was that many of the differences in the speech of men and women – even differences in pitch – could not be explained entirely by reference to biological differences. Social codes play an even more fundamental role in constructing gender identities, including a gendered linguistic identity. Part of this identity is based on expectations of appropriate behaviour for both women and men, which vary from one society to another and also from one period in history to another.

The process of acquiring the norms of behaviour in society begins early. One of the first questions asked of parents on the birth of their children is, 'Is it a boy or a girl?' From then on, people respond differently to children on the basis of the initial categorisation by sex, and thus begins the gender acquisition process. Since 'gender' is acquired rather than innate, it refers to the rules of behaviour which we learn as part of the society in which we grow up. These rules vary from one society to another, but sex differences are biologically based. Consequently, when discussing linguistic differences, the term 'gender' rather than 'sex' is used to indicate that what is being discussed is a socially-constructed category.

Another important point to bear in mind when discussing 'gender' is that linguists may use the term 'gender' with another meaning, that of 'grammatical gender', which refers to the ways in which words are divided into categories in some languages, such as French and German (although not English), which are said to have 'masculine gender' or 'feminine gender'.[34] Such uses are quite distinct from the use of the word 'gender' as a social category in this book, and in others dealing with socio-linguistic topics.

An interesting aspect of gender variation, in contrast

to some other types of variation, is the fact that women and men communicate freely, without restriction, with each other in most societies. In other words, differences in their speech patterns cannot be explained by lack of linguistic contact in the way that one might explain geographical or social class variation. Since men and women interact with each other in all – or most – social contexts, explanations of gender differences have to be sought elsewhere.

It is important too to remember that differences between how women and men speak (in English) are not sex-exclusive, but sex-preferential. In other words, identified differences are not confined to one sex to the exclusion of the other. There is only a tendency for them to be used by members of one sex. No form of language has been identified in English which is used only by women or men. It is true too that not all women share the traits that are said to characterise the speech of their sex and that men may use these traits also. Gay men, for example, may use features more commonly associated with women's speech.

MALE-AS-NORM
Research in Sociolinguistics during recent decades has established without question that there has been a male bias in documenting and explaining gender differences in language. This bias is manifest in various ways, going back to how variation in language was studied by grammarians and dialectologists in the early part of the twentieth century.

One fact to note is that early researchers and fieldworkers in the study of dialects (dialectology) were mostly men and so the development of research strategies and tools was directed very much from a male perspective. When dialectologists were studying dialects, their objective was to record and document them before the dialects died out, and they chose mostly male informants. This is established as fact rather than as anecdote by data quoted in Jennifer Coates's *Women, Men and Language* (1993), which reveals the proportion of women informants in various dialect surveys internationally between 1902 and 1978. The surveys were carried out in France, Catalonia, Southern Austria, Italy, Switzerland, Sardinia, Corsica, Belgian Congo, North China and England. The number of women informants varies from 0 per cent (Belgian Congo) to 20.45 per cent (Southern Austria).[35] Even the highest figure represents a serious under-representation of a group which comprises roughly half the world's population. It is obvious from this lack of recourse to women as informants that men were considered the main custodians of language.

Male bias is also evident in the choice of vocabulary items included in the questionnaires used by dialectologists. Coates (1993) describes the situation as follows:

One of the reasons women were not used as informants was that (male) dialectologists defined which areas of life and therefore which lexical sets were worthy of study from an essentially androcentric point of view.[36]

Looking at the lists of topics chosen as quoted by Coates, it is abundantly clear that dialectologists viewed the world from a very male point of view, with women being added on only peripherally. In a list of thirty-one topics from a questionnaire used in France, which included everything from 'the vineyard' to 'the body', there are only two items which refer specifically to women:

Women's life: 1. The bed, housekeeping, meals
Women's life: 2. Washing, sewing [37]

Presumably it was thought that men would not be familiar, or at least not as familiar or knowledgeable as women, with these topics, so fieldworkers resorted to women to fill the gaps. All the other topics in the questionnaire are not categorised according to gender, and so, as male informants were the norm, there was no need to specify that men would be providing the data. From a late-twentieth-century perspective, there seems to be no reason why women should not have been used more systematically in the survey as informants in relation to all categories. Nevertheless, in the early part of the century, access to men as interviewees would have been easier, and husbands might not have liked their wives spending time with some strange male scholar! The fact that 'women's life' is referred to as a special category in the surveys only confirms that, in the social – and consequently linguistic – situation that obtained at the time, men, not women, were the point of reference or the norm.

A famous – or by now infamous – example of male bias is to be found in a chapter entitled 'The Woman', in

Language: Its Nature, Development and Origin, published in 1922 by a respected linguist, Otto Jespersen. On the positive side, Jespersen does at least see the merit of describing women's language and he does give an account of discussion on the subject up to that time, with reference to a variety of languages including Sanskrit and Japanese. On a more negative note, what he has to say about women's language is very much biased towards interpreting it as a more restricted form of the language exhibited by men. For instance, he suggests that women's vocabulary is much less extensive than men's and that women are less likely than men to invent or use new words:

> The vocabulary of a woman is much less extensive than that of a man. Women move preferably in the central field of language, avoiding everything that is out of the way or bizarre, while men will often either coin new words or expressions or take up old-fashioned ones, if by that means they are enabled, or think they are enabled, to find a more adequate or precise expression for their thoughts.[38]

Nowadays it would be unusual to come across such sexist and male bias. More recent work investigating gender differences does not display the same blatant bias against women. Sociolinguists now employ more scientific methods of choosing samples for analysis, and the methods used by traditional dialectologists would no longer be considered acceptable or reliable. Notwithstanding the improvements in the inclusion of women as informants, there are still issues which remain to be resolved in the collection of data in the field of language. Many of the classic studies in Sociolinguistics, for example by William Labov in the USA and Peter Trudgill in England, were carried out by upper-middle-class male academics. It is accepted now that the fact that the researchers were male had an effect on the data provided by women informants. It is still not unheard of to come across conclusions about language in general drawn from analysis of the speech of men only, whereas general conclusions about language would never be drawn from information gleaned exclusively from the speech of women informants.

Feminist linguists continue to point out the various shortcomings of supposedly objective scientific research. Questions have been raised about the assignment of married women to social categories on the basis of their husband's occupation, rather than on the basis of criteria such as women's own level of education. Deborah Cameron, in particular, in her book *Feminism and Linguistic Theory* (1985), expresses many reservations about, for example, the unquestioned acceptance of men's speech patterns as the 'norm' from which women 'deviate'. The underlying message of the 'male-as-norm' situation is that what men speak is 'real' language and that what women speak is a form of language which diverges from, and is defined in relation to, the norm represented by men. Although we have come some way since the beginning of the twentieth century, we have not yet reached a situation of true equality of treatment in this area, no more than in many others.

CONCLUSION

Language varies in relation to a number of criteria, one of which is gender. However, until recent years and in particular until the feminist movement emerged, gender difference was inadequately described and poorly understood. Many shortcomings have been identified in early methods used to identify how this type of variation is actualised in speech. Even modern methods, despite their adherence to objective research principles, still operate in a male-as-norm paradigm, which relegates women's speech patterns to the category of deviation from the norm. Considering women's speech patterns as of secondary importance is hardly appropriate when women constitute more than 50 per cent of the world's population.

The next two chapters will examine more closely various aspects of gender differences in language use.

4

GENDER DIFFERENCES IN LANGUAGE USE: 'TALKING PROPER'

FEATURES OF WOMEN'S LANGUAGE

When Robin Lakoff's book *Language and Woman's Place* was published in 1975, it set the agenda in the field of language and gender studies for some time to come.[39] She examined many of the stereotypes and conventional beliefs about women's speech and drew conclusions about them based on her own experiences and intuition. Many linguists used her work as a starting point for their own work and subsequently tested empirically some of the assertions she made. Much controversy has ensued about her conclusions and also about the fact that they were based, not on field work, but on her own intuition. Many subsequent studies attempted to test her hypotheses, using more rigorous sociolinguistic methodologies.

Of course there is not universal agreement about whether or not gender differences actually exist in language. Some commentators believe that supposed gender differences are exaggerated and exploited by the feminist movement with the objective of drawing attention to the role of language as another indicator of the socially disadvantaged position of women. Most researchers in the field have worked to prove the assumption, following in the tradition established by Lakoff, that there are marked gender differences. Many continue the analysis further by pursuing the issue of the social consequences for women of linguistic differentiation. Others have undertaken research on sociolinguistic issues such as socio-economic class differences and realised that gender was at least an equally important consideration as social background. One thing is certain: research done in the last thirty years or so proves conclusively that gender differences do exist. Trudgill (1983b) – a sociolinguist who could hardly be accused of advancing a feminist agenda – concludes on this point emphatically:

> It is absolutely clear, however, that the evidence provided by sociolinguistic studies for sex differences in language is utterly overwhelming. *It is the single most consistent finding to emerge from sociolinguistic work in the past two decades.* Some people may regard the existence of this phenomenon as embarrassing or undesirable, but there is absolutely no doubt that it does exist.[40] (Emphasis added)

The issue is then no longer to debate the existence of gender differences, but for linguists to attempt to describe them accurately and comprehensively. The next step is to seek explanations.

The features Lakoff identified as characterising women's

speech fall mainly into the categories of vocabulary and syntax (or grammar). In her book *Talking Power: The Politics of Language* (1990), she gives an even more detailed list than she does in *Language and Woman's Place* of what she considers to be the features of women's language and provides an interpretation of the reasons for and consequences of this differentiation. A possible unifying characteristic of the linguistic features identified by Lakoff is the explanation she gives: she believes that the features she identifies as belonging to women's language indicate tentativeness, uncertainty, lack of conviction or lack of confidence. In the following subsections I will examine the facts relating to the various aspects of women's speech that have been the subject of extensive study.

Pronunciation

There are no examples of languages where women and men use completely different sound systems, for obvious reasons – comprehension between speakers would be rather problematic. Equally, there are few examples of languages where men and women use different sounds in some contexts. Usually the entire range of sounds is available to both sexes, as is the case in English, although there may be variation in how they are used in practice. In order to find examples of sounds which are used exclusively by one sex or the other, you have to look to non-Western languages.

In Sociolinguistics textbooks, one of the most frequently quoted examples of a situation where men use one sound and women use a different one in the same context is the case of the Gros Ventre American Indians in

Montana. In Gros Ventre, men use /dj/ in contexts where women use /kj/. For example, the men say /dja'tsa/ for 'bread' and the women say /kja'tsa/.[41] Another example comes from Yukaghir, a northeast Asian language, where the sounds /ts/ and /dz/ for women correspond, respectively, to /tj/ and dj/ for men. This difference in Yukaghir is also connected to age differences, since children use the female forms and old people of both sexes use another set altogether. In Bengali (a language of India), women use /l/ at the beginning of some words, where men use /n/.[42]

In Western communities, differentiation at the level of pronunciation is not obvious. There are no sounds which are used exclusively by either men or women. What has been identified, however, is the fact that gender variation in sound results from women and men using different frequencies or quantities of sounds which they have in common. Much of this information has come from studies whose initial objective was to study social class differences but which also showed conclusively that gender was an extremely significant factor in patterns of variation. Sociolinguists who carry out research on features of language which show this kind of variation refer to them as 'sociolinguistic variables'. Many of the variables studied are in the area of pronunciation or accent differences, which have provided a lot of valuable evidence on how language shows gender differences in practice. Some of the most studied sociolinguistic variables are:

- use of the -in' ending as opposed to the -ing ending, in words like 'walking' and 'running', which are then pronounced as if they were spelt 'walkin' and 'runnin'.

- whether or not *r* is pronounced after a vowel, for example in words like 'car' and 'door'.
- presence or absence of *h* in, for example, 'head' or 'house'.
- how *t* is pronounced in words like 'bet' and 'butter'.[43]

Data on these variables were collected systematically in New York by William Labov (1966; 1972a; 1972b), in Detroit by Wolfram (1969), and in Norwich, England, by Trudgill (1974; 1983a; 1983b). The conclusions in most cases were that women tended to use the more prestigious variable – they tended to say 'walking' and 'running' rather than 'walkin' and 'runnin', for example – more frequently than men. This finding has led to all sorts of statements being made about women's speech patterns being more 'correct' or closer to the standard forms than those of men, who tend to use more 'non-standard', vernacular, spoken forms.

The finding that women tend to use more prestigious forms of speech relates not just to pronunciation but also to various grammatical features. For example, women have been shown to use double negatives (e.g., 'I didn't say nothing'; 'I didn't tell no one') less frequently than men.[44] Other features which have been examined include the use of 'ain't' and the use of the past participle as the past tense, as in 'I seen' or 'I done', and the findings from numerous studies which have been carried out internationally show overwhelmingly that women use the standard form more frequently than men. Thus, there is an established pattern of women talking 'more proper' than men.

GENDER AND PRESTIGE

In Trudgill's survey of speech in Norwich, England, informants were asked to participate in a self-evaluation test investigating what they thought they said as opposed to what they actually did say as noted by the researchers. An interesting fact thrown up by the test is that women reported that they used standard forms more frequently than they actually did and men reported that they used them less frequently than they actually did. Trudgill puts it like this when describing the pronunciation of the vowel in the words 'ear' and 'here', which has two main variants in Norwich:

> ... a majority of women reported themselves as using RP [Received Pronunciation] /ɪə/ when in fact they did not ... as many as half the men went the other way and under-reported – they reported themselves as using a less statusful, more lower-class form than they normally used.[45]

The terms 'prestige' and 'prestige variety' are used by linguists such as Labov and Trudgill to refer to the fact that some forms of language enjoy higher standing in their linguistic community than others. For example, in English-speaking communities, saying 'running' rather than 'runnin' has more prestige, because it is regarded as more 'standard' or more 'correct'. This kind of prestige is often called 'overt prestige'. So, women are described as using forms of language (e.g., 'running') which have 'overt prestige' more frequently than men. On the other hand, men have been found to use forms (e.g., 'runnin') which are described as having 'covert prestige'. In other words, they use forms which are more characteristic of spoken language, which do not enjoy 'overt prestige', but which derive their prestige from the fact that they are shared by members of a particular social group and so have connotations of group solidarity. This is especially true, it is suggested, among members of working-class groups. The term 'covert' is used since this kind of prestige comes from attitudes which are not usually overtly expressed because they are at variance with the more mainstream values in society (represented by institutions such as schools) associated with 'overt prestige'.

Various explanations have been advanced in an attempt to explain why women should show greater attachment to high prestige forms and why men should show preference for non-standard forms. Trudgill's (1983b) explanation of this phenomenon in the speech patterns of Norwich is that men use non-standard 'covert prestige' forms because 'working class speech has favourable connotations for male speakers' in that it expresses male solidarity and is therefore a badge of group identity.[46] A member of such a group might be accused of attempting to speak 'posh', by using forms with 'overt prestige', and be laughed at or ostracised.

It has often been said (for example by Trudgill) that women are more conservative and more status-conscious than men and therefore they prefer established 'correct' forms. This explanation is rather controversial and is based on the idea that, since many women operate in the private sphere as homemakers, they are more dependent on factors other than occupation, such as appearance and speech patterns, for indicating their social status. John Honey, in *Language is Power: The Story of Standard and its Enemies* (1997), articulates a form of this argument when he suggests that women use standard forms as a 'power-sharing' or 'power-grabbing' exercise – to which he attributes positive value.

> There is now an abundance of convincing evidence – from Britain, the United States, and a wide range of other countries and cultures – that women outdo men in tending to use standard forms of language, especially grammar and accent. Prominent among several factors that may be at work here is the awareness – conscious or unconscious – that, in societies characterised by male dominance, this constitutes a subtle method of grasping a small share of that power.[47]

The information on over-reporting referred to at the beginning of this section seems to support the argument for the 'status-consciousness of women', but it is not conclusive. A study done by Lesley Milroy (1980) showed that a group of working-class women in Belfast favoured non-standard forms rather than the prestige norms that might have been expected on earlier evidence. Milroy's explanation is based on the notion of 'social network', which characterises closely-knit groups of women just as much as the groups of men in Trudgill's study of Norwich.

Another possible explanation can be found in society's expectations of women's behaviour. Women are generally expected to behave 'better' than men and therefore departure from norms in women is more frowned upon. For example, overindulgence in alcohol is even more unacceptable in women than it is in men, and women who commit violent crimes are regarded as a complete aberration, as women are considered to be 'gentle' and 'feminine' by nature. Speech patterns are an integral part of society's expectations of politeness and good behaviour in women, especially in the context of showing example to the members of the next generation in their care. Consequently, 'talking proper' may be seen as a kind of moral obligation which women are required to assume more than men, since society still expects them to take greater responsibility for bringing up children.

Other explanations for women preferring more 'correct' forms have focused on such issues as the influence of those collecting the data. It is likely too that women adapt their speech patterns to those of their middle-class interviewers. It is a normal process in language to vary linguistic features according to the social context (see Chapter 3). The fact that women display more cooperative patterns in conversation may also be a factor in their accommodating to the kind of language used by their interviewers (see Chapter 5). There may also be distortion because of the assignment of women to social classes based on their husband's occupation.

None of the explanations advanced is, of itself, conclusive and much remains to be done to find adequate and convincing explanations for confirmed differences in gender speech patterns.[48] What is certain is that the relationship between gender and prestige in language is a complex one, not amenable to quick conclusions or simple explanations.

PITCH AND INTONATION

One of the issues involved in studying gender differences in pronunciation is pitch – the level of the voice, whether high or low. Pitch is of interest since it appears to be a 'sex' rather than a 'gender' characteristic. Conventional wisdom suggests that women speak at a higher pitch than men because of differences in physiology. While the basis of this assertion is true, recent work has shown that differences in pitch can be exaggerated and that this may happen as part of the process of acquiring norms appropriate to a particular gender.

Pitch and intonation in language are closely connected, since intonation is the result of variation in pitch. No one speaks in a monotone in the way that early versions of robots and voice simulators did; all speakers go up and down in pitch as they speak. These variations are exploited for communicative purposes by language as a way of distinguishing meaning. An obvious example of variation in pitch to indicate a particular meaning is the rise in pitch, or 'rising intonation', which is used to signal that the speaker is asking a question. Conversely, statements which are declaring something (called 'declarative statements' or simply 'declaratives') are usually characterised by a drop in pitch or 'falling intonation'.

Pitch is produced by the vibration of the vocal chords

in the larynx (sometimes known as 'the voice box'). When you breathe out, as air comes up from the lungs, through the windpipe, the vocal chords can be brought together and the air pushes against the vocal chords causing them to vibrate and produce sound. The basic rate of vibration of the vocal chords is the most important aspect of pitch. Thick, heavy vocal chords vibrate more slowly than lighter ones and since men tend to have thicker, heavier vocal chords than women, they tend to produce lower pitch. Consequently, there are physiological explanations for the differences in pitch between women and men.

Graddol and Swann in *Gender Voices* (1989) refer to evidence that differences in pitch are subject to social learning.[49] It is obvious that men or women can adjust the pitch of their voices upwards or downwards in a conscious way. A conspicuous example is Margaret Thatcher, who lowered her pitch after she became Prime Minister of Britain.[50] There are also many examples of male actors playing the roles of women, some of the best known on film being Jack Lemmon and Tony Curtis in *Some Like it Hot* and, more recently, Dustin Hoffman in *Tootsie* and Robin Williams in *Mrs Doubtfire*. While it is possible to vary pitch dramatically in this way, it might not be very comfortable over extended periods. However, Graddol and Swann point to the large degree of overlap that exists between the average range of women's voices and the average range of men's voices. The lower range of women's voices overlaps considerably with the higher range of men's voices, so there is no absolute cut-off point between them. Graddol and Swann refer to a study they carried out in 1983, which produced the following results, supporting the view that there is more than physiology to pitch:

> The comparison shows that people can place their voice ranges somewhat flexibly. For some reason, the men and women in our study were adopting different strategies. Men's voices reflected their physical size because they used the lower limits of their pitch range and adopted intonation patterns which were more monotonous than women's; women by contrast, were more variable in their use of voice, both in the sense of using expressive intonation and in differences between individual women. Such differences seem to indicate that pitch of voice carries social meanings and that men and women try to communicate different social images.[51]

Graddol and Swann develop the point further by discussing evidence of the fact that boys' and girls' voices can be distinguished well before puberty, i.e., the time at which sex differences come into play.[52] There is also evidence that pitch is culturally variable. Thus, the proposition can hardly be sustained that pitch is wholly and entirely determined by purely physical features. There is a strong cultural element involved and people, even youngsters, learn patterns of pitch appropriate to their gender in the linguistic community to which they belong.

The evidence from Graddol and Swann's study confirms some of what Robin Lakoff (1975; 1990) identified as features of women's language in the area of intonation. Lakoff states that:

- Women's intonational contours display more variety than men's.
- Women use intonation patterns that resemble questions, indicating uncertainty or need for approval.
- Women's voices are breathier than men's.[53]

It seems as if women do use a greater variety and range of intonation patterns than men and this appears to form part of the expectations of the linguistic behaviour of women in English. A well known example of what is considered desirable in a woman's voice comes from the Shakespearean character King Lear, who complimented his daughter Cordelia by saying that:

> Her voice was soft,
> Gentle and low, an excellent thing in woman.[54]

The disadvantage for women of using high pitch as well as a greater range of pitch is that high pitch is associated with overexcitement and hysteria and low pitch with authority. These features (low pitch and variety of pitch), which appear to be – at least to some extent – learnt, probably contribute to some of the negative stereotypes of women as 'excitable' and 'overemotional'. Since women's higher-pitched voices are not taken as seriously as lower-pitched male voices, many women alter their pitch and reduce the amount of variation in pitch, if they want to succeed in male-dominated environments. Standard advice to women in this context is that, to maintain gravitas, they should speak in as low and controlled a voice as possible. Margaret Thatcher's lowering of the pitch (and presumably the range) of her voice rid her of any possibility of being regarded as a 'hysterical female' and enhanced the image she wanted to project of authority, calmness and rationality. In the case of newscasters, too, high voices are not considered 'serious', so more men tend to feature as newsreaders and in 'serious' current affairs programmes. The women newsreaders who do feature in the media tend to have rather low-pitched voices. Because of the association between low pitch and seriousness and authority, who would believe the news bulletins if they were delivered in a very high-pitched voice?

The 'breathiness' to which Lakoff refers affects voice quality and results from another process which may take place in the vocal chords. A voice is 'breathy' if the vocal chords do not close fully when they vibrate, allowing more air or 'breath' to get through. An extreme example of a 'breathy' voice is that used by Lorelei Lee, the character played by Marilyn Monroe in the film version of the Anita Loos book *Gentlemen Prefer Blondes.* Various studies indicate that 'breathiness' is associated with female voices, including one quoted by Graddol and Swann which showed that, in two British accents, women consistently used a 'breathier' voice quality than men.[55]

Of course there is nothing inherently negative about either high pitch or 'breathiness'. The fact is that negative connotations have become associated with them. Deborah Cameron in her book *Feminism and Linguistic Theory* (1985) suggests that the fact alone that women use a particular feature is enough for it to be viewed negatively:

If men talked in higher pitches than women, low voices would be said to lack in authority ... Linguistic sex-differences act simply as a badge of femaleness, and are valued negatively quite irrespective of their substance.[56]

QUESTIONS AND ANSWERS

Another feature which Lakoff describes as characterising women's speech is the use of rising intonation patterns which have the effect of making statements resemble questions.[57] Women tend to use the rising intonation of a question, where one might expect the falling intonation of a declarative (statement). She gives the following example of a verbal exchange between a man (a) and a woman (b):

(a) 'When will dinner be ready?'
(b) 'Oh ... around six o'clock?'[58]

She suggests that, instead of giving an answer to the question in statement form, a woman is more likely to give the answer in question form, as if she is checking for approval from the addressee or as if she is unsure of herself (even although she may be the only person with the relevant information!). This assertion on the part of Lakoff is somewhat controversial as is her related claim that women use more 'tag-questions' (a question added on to a declarative) than men – she cautions that she does not have statistical evidence to back up the claim. The following are examples of two very common question types, with the 'tags' underlined:

It's a nice day, <u>isn't it</u>?

That was a great film, <u>wasn't it</u>?

Since a tag-question is 'midway between an outright statement and a 'yes-no' question, it is less assertive than the former, but more confident than the latter', Lakoff suggests that it is used as a means –

> whereby a speaker can avoid committing himself, and thereby avoid coming into conflict with the addressee. The problem is that, by so doing, a speaker may also give the impression of not being really sure of himself, of looking to the addressee for confirmation, even of having no views of his own.[59]

In other words, for Lakoff, tag-questions are associated with lack of assertiveness, a characteristic which is regularly applied to women. They can also be seen as a form of politeness strategy (which we will investigate further in the next chapter) since, by using them, the speaker includes and involves the addressee in the interaction more than would be the case if bald statements were made. Saying 'That was a great film, wasn't it?' encourages the addressee to proffer an opinion, whereas 'That was a great film' is a more conclusive statement.

This claim regarding women's use of tag-questions has been investigated extensively since it was first put forward by Lakoff. Studies have not been conclusive on whether or not women use them more than men. Some studies have corroborated Lakoff's finding. Others have proved the opposite. One aptly entitled 'The Question of Tag-Questions in Women's Speech: They Don't Really Use More Of Them, Do They?' proved that men used more. [60]

There is now general agreement that tag-questions may have many functions. For example, a person in authority, such as a teacher, might ask a pupil: 'You could have done better, couldn't you?' While this usage might seek confirmation on the part of the addressee, it certainly does not indicate lack of conviction or lack of assertiveness on the part of the speaker.

Deborah Cameron (1985) concludes on the tag-question issue as follows:

1. Women do not use more tag-questions than men.
2. Even if they did, it would not necessarily mean that they were looking for approval, since tag-questions have a range of uses.
3. In any case, women's use of tag-questions will always be explained differently from men's, since it is cultural sex stereotypes which determine the explanation of linguistic phenomena, rather than the nature of the phenomena themselves.[61]

Despite the fact that Lakoff's claim about tag-questions turned out to be unfounded, it has passed into the folklore about women's linguistic behaviour and has become a stereotype, a kind of 'linguistic stereotype'. Tag-questions are often mentioned in popular descriptions as a characteristic of women's speech and they feature in magazine articles giving advice to women on what they should avoid in terms of linguistic behaviour, all despite the fact that there is little supporting evidence on the point.[62]

CONCLUSION

All the evidence of the past few decades, since people began to look seriously at the issue of whether or not women and men 'speak the same language', indicates that there are quite a lot of differences in the ways both groups use language. As we have seen, there are no examples in English of forms which are used exclusively by one gender or the other, there are only tendencies for forms which they have in common to be used more frequently by one gender than the other. The over-whelming truth is that women talk more 'properly' than men, all other things (such as social class) being equal. If one form of pronunciation, or feature of grammar, is considered more 'correct' and therefore more prestigious than another, then women will tend to use it more frequently than men of the same social class. This contributes to the perception that women are more 'polite', a view which is also supported by features of vocabulary and behaviour in conversation, which we will look at in the next chapter.

5

GENDER DIFFERENCES IN LANGUAGE USE: 'LOOK WHO'S NOT TALKING!'

TABOO WORDS

One of the cultural stereotypes about women's speech is that women do not use taboo words of various kinds, such as swear words or crude language. It is not considered 'ladylike' for a woman to swear and men often apologise for using strong language in the presence of 'ladies'. Not only, then, is it not expected that 'ladies' should use vulgar language themselves, they are expected to be horrified when it is used by others, and they are supposed to react as if their 'delicate constitution' has been offended by it.

While restrictions on what is considered appropriate for women to say in Western societies usually involve obscenities and profanities, in some non-Western societies restrictions on what women are allowed to say can go further. For example, women may be forbidden from using the names of their husband's male relatives, or other words which resemble the names affected by this taboo. Trudgill (1983b) points out that it appears to be the case in Zulu that this prohibition could go so far as to include forbidding the use of certain sounds contained in the tabooed words.[63]

While this situation does not obtain in Western languages, there are still expectations about what is suitable or appropriate for women to say and not to say. Nonetheless, tolerance levels have changed a lot over recent decades. What was considered inappropriate for our mothers and grandmothers is less unacceptable now. With social roles of women and men converging more and more, there is also convergence in speech patterns, and this includes changes in what is considered appropriate vocabulary. Consequently, it has become more common for women – at least for younger women – to use vulgar language. To some, this seems like a negative consequence of equality. There are still constraints in older age groups, where swearing would be more frowned upon, so women who might swear when speaking to other people their own age would moderate this tendency when speaking to people of older age groups. This would also happen when they are speaking to children, when swear words are much less likely to occur. In other words, the use of swear words would be another example of style-shifting, which was discussed in Chapter 3.

COLOUR TERMS AND HOUSEHOLD WORDS

As well as words and phrases which women are not expected to use – or are expected to use less than men – some words are more associated with women than men. In *Language and Woman's Place* (1975), Robin Lakoff refers to the greater use of some areas of vocabulary by women, such as colour terms and terms associated with 'women's spheres of interest'. Words associated with the private sphere, with activities like sewing and knitting, would be more widely known and used by women but much less likely to be used by men. How many men would know what colour 'magenta' is, that 'darts' mean something other than the name of a game, or that 'piping' is a kind of edging found on cushions and upholstery, not just something used in heating and plumbing? How many men would have ever heard – let alone know the meaning – of 'cross-stitch', 'purl', 'lazy-daisy', 'cable' or 'blackberry stitch'? Of course, fewer and fewer women are familiar with them too, since there has been a decline in activities like sewing, knitting and craft work in general but, on average, it is still true that women are far more likely to be familiar with these terms than men are.

Lakoff asserts that:

Women . . . make far more precise discriminations in naming colours than do men; words like beige, ecru, aquamarine, lavender, and so on are unremarkable in a woman's vocabulary, but absent from that of most men.[64]

The reason for women's greater knowledge of colour terms can probably be related to traditional views of women as being more concerned with the private domain, i.e., having an interest in home decoration and clothes. Of course men who work in the fashion industry would, by virtue of their work, be obliged to have fine colour discrimination and presumably an attendant ability to describe colour accurately. Funnily enough, one rarely hears praise for someone who has a wide vocabulary of colour terms, or indeed terms related to sewing and knitting. Possessing a wide vocabulary is, generally, a reason to be admired, but somehow, colour terms do not really seem to count for very much in this context. If anything, arguing over the correct colour term (e.g., over whether something is fawn or beige) would probably be seen as trivial. It seems that when something is associated with women, that is enough to downgrade it. There are, however, good reasons why a refined colour vocabulary should be considered an advantage, an obvious one being the ability to provide precise information about colour of clothing or cars, in the context of police investigations. Colour discrimination is essential too in the natural world and in medicine.

TENTATIVENESS AND POLITENESS

In *Language and Power* (1990), Lakoff details some of the features she considers to be typical of women's vocabulary:

- Women make more use of expressive forms (adjectives not nouns or verbs and, in that category, those expressing emotional rather than intellectual evaluation) more than men: lovely, divine.
- Women use hedges of all kinds more than men.
- Women use diminutives and euphemisms more than men.[65]

She suggests that there are neutral adjectives, which may

be used by either men or women, like 'great, terrific, cool, neat,' and adjectives which are used by women only, such as 'adorable, charming, sweet, lovely, divine.[66] As a result, women could say either of the following sentences, whereas men could only use the first one, if they were not to be laughed at:

That's a great plan!
That's a divine plan!

The second sentence would be considered effeminate, and rather theatrical, especially if accompanied by the great variation in pitch and intonation which was discussed in the previous chapter. This combination of 'feminine' vocabulary and intonation is often associated with gay men and flamboyant performers such as Julian Clary in Britain, who exaggerates these features for effect.

Women's greater use of hedges and euphemisms can be identified with more general social strategies which have been associated with women, such as 'politeness' and 'ladylike behaviour'. 'Hedges' are ways of softening statements, making them less direct, more non-committal, using words and phrases like: 'sort of', 'kind of', 'I think', 'perhaps' and 'you know', in sentences like:

That's sort of difficult to say.
I think that film was kind of interesting.
Perhaps we might try this another way.
It was, you know, really good.

Many studies have been done on 'hedging devices' and it is not possible to give one simple answer to the questions of when, how and how often they are used, and whether or not women use them more than men, or with the same objectives. There is a problem with isolating particular features (such as hedging devices like 'you know') from their context and analysing them as if there is only one possible interpretation of their function (e.g., as an indication of powerlessness). There is so much individual variation on features like 'hedges', that it is difficult to generalise conclusively about this kind of gender difference.[67]

Euphemisms are, basically, a 'nice' way of saying unpleasant things. For example, instead of saying someone has died, it is common for people to avoid using the word 'death' baldly, by replacing it with another more indirect word. Examples of euphemisms for 'dying' in English are:

Parting
Departure
Passing
Passing on
Passing away
End
Loss
Going to one's reward[68]

If women use euphemisms more than men, this could be interpreted as a politeness strategy, a way of being nice to people and avoiding giving offence.[69] More material needs to be gathered in order to provide conclusive evidence of gender differences in these and related areas. In the meantime, much attention has been given to attempting to understand how these features fit into the broader question of how politeness – especially as demonstrated by women – is represented linguistically.

COMMUNICATIVE COMPETENCE AND COMMUNICATIVE STYLES

Politeness strategies as features of the linguistic behaviour of women have attracted a lot of attention recently, as interest has grown in the influence of gender on not just the smaller 'chunks' of language but on larger 'chunks', such as complete conversations or formal meetings. There had been a tendency in Linguistics to concentrate on the basic elements of language, such as features of pronunciation, vocabulary and grammar and, consequently, to overlook the more social aspects of language and the ways in which language is used in different contexts for different communicative purposes. In recent years, the balance has been redressed significantly, with the growth in interest and relevance of the field of Discourse Analysis, which looks at how larger chunks of language are used in different contexts, such as in advertising, journalism, the workplace and informal conversation. Not surprisingly, these areas have provided a wealth of information about language use and how it varies from one communicative situation to another. This information is not just useful and interesting for linguists, it is also of great interest and relevance to the general public.

When people learn to speak a language, they learn the

'nuts and bolts' of their particular first language; in other words, they gain what is called 'linguistic competence', which includes the various levels that linguists identify as the major components of language: phonology (sound structure), morphology (word structure), syntax (sentence structure) and lexis (vocabulary). It is now accepted that this is only the starting point for effective language use. If people did not know, for example, how to conduct conversations appropriately in their socio-cultural group, all the grammatical knowledge in the world would be insufficient for them to be accepted as successful speakers of their language. For example, people would react badly if, during a conversation, someone kept talking at the same time as another speaker, remained silent when asked a question or looked out the window instead of looking at the person speaking. All of these things involve linguistic knowledge as well as knowledge of the norms of conversational behaviour and some knowledge of appropriate paralinguistic behaviour. So, speaking a language necessitates not only knowledge of grammar in its widest sense, it also requires knowledge of how to interact with other speakers in an acceptable way, following unwritten, conventional rules, which vary from one society to another. This kind of comprehensive knowledge of how to behave in a particular language setting is called 'communicative competence'.

It has been widely suggested that women's communicative competence is different from men's and that, consequently, they have a different communicative style from men. In other words, they adopt different approaches to verbal interaction in a wide variety of contexts from private conversations to group meetings. In recent years, various topics have been selected and analysed with the objective of describing the characteristics of talk, and how it differs in relation to gender, in various circumstances. Of all the areas which have attracted attention in terms of gender behaviour, the area of conversation has been the most prolific and also the one which has given rise to the greatest amount of controversy among specialists in Linguistics and the interested public. Some of the topics which have attracted attention are:

- Conversational dominance – who occupies most of the talking time.
- Turn-taking – how participants get their turns to speak, and how and why they give them up.
- Interruption – who interrupts who and when (e.g., without waiting for a turn to be completed).
- Topic selection – who gets to choose the topics, i.e., those which get discussed and those which do not.
- General conversational strategies – such as politeness and inclusiveness.

Silence (Ladies) Please!

Probably the most astonishing finding of the many studies carried out over the last few decades is that, contrary to the cultural stereotype that women speak a lot (too much?), women do not speak more than men in mixed-sex situations and men interrupt women far more frequently than the other way round. In 1997, Canadian Prime Minister Jean Chrétien was able to impress a gathering of Liberal women with his grasp of this important fact by announcing that he had known for thirty-four years that 'women work harder and talk less' and that was why he always employed a woman to run his constituency office.[70]

Generalisations about gender differences in amount of talking time need to be nuanced in relation to the social situation in which the interaction is taking place. There is quite an amount of difference depending on whether the social context is public or private. As a general rule, the more public the forum, the less likely women are to occupy an equal amount of the talking time, or even to speak at all. In a public forum, such as a committee meeting, women are likely to speak less than men. Robin Lakoff describes a typical committee meeting at the University of California at Berkeley, explaining her frustration at the amount of time which was being taken up with talk which seemed to be getting nowhere, and which could be summarised in a sentence:

> I would attempt to provide that sentence. But once I had spoken, the discourse would close over me like the ocean enveloping a pebble. It was as if I had not spoken – in fact, did not exist. What did it mean? After a while I figured it out. My colleagues were playing by men's rules: what was important was to gain turf, control territory. That goal was achieved by spreading words around.[71]

Even in less public, less formal contexts, it seems that women do not talk as much as men, despite their reputation for being verbose. If anything, there is an unwritten assumption that men are somehow more entitled to talk and be listened to than women, and that, in any case, what men have to say is more interesting and more important. Imagine the following dinner party scenarios. In the first instance, only the men are talking and the women are not (they are presumably listening to what the men are saying). In the second case, the women are talking and the men are not. Which scenario is more expected and more acceptable socially? You do not have to think about it for long, as the answer is obvious. In the first case the party would be thought to be going well, but in the second case, when women are holding the floor, the hosts might worry that the party was not going well. As Gloria Steinem puts it:

Check the talk politics concealed in your own behaviour. Does your anxiety level go up (and your hostess instincts quiver?) when women are talking and men are listening, but not the reverse? For instance, men often seem to feel okay about 'talking shop' while women listen, but women seem able to talk in men's presence for only a short time before feeling anxious, apologising, and encouraging the men to speak.[72]

Since Dale Spender described women as a 'muted' group in *Man Made Language* (1980), the issue of women's silence has come to the fore. Spender's view is that women have been silenced, deprived of their voice and their right to speak, not only metaphorically, but literally. We saw when discussing proverbs in Chapter 1 that silence is regarded – at least proverbially – as a desirable state for a woman. There are also social occasions when it is usual for men to have all the speaking parts. A very ritualised and stylised form of this is evident in 'wedding reception etiquette', where the groom, best man, father of the bride (and possibly other men such as officiating clergy) make speeches. Up until recently it was very unusual for women to take part in the formal speeches at all, although it is becoming more common now for the bride to speak.[73]

When they are picking up gender norms, it seems likely that girls learn that they are not expected to hold the floor as much as boys and the expectation is built up that males somehow have more control over who has the right to speak. Most people would deny this claim vehemently, but the evidence from investigations on the subject is very enlightening and very conclusive. Various studies point out the discrepancy between what proportion of 'talking time' we think women take up as opposed to men and what the reality of the situation is. It seems that we are very bad at judging proportions of talking time. Even when women and men talk for approximately the same time, observers are under the impression that the women have talked more. Fortunately, current research makes use of video recording equipment which measures accurately the amount of time each speaker takes up, so results are based on fact rather than impression. When Myra and David Sadker recorded a classroom discussion in 1985, teachers looking at the film thought that the girls talked more than the boys, whereas in reality, the boys talked three times as much. Similar problems of perception of talking time were reported by many other writers, including Carole Edelsky in her article 'Who's Got the Floor?' (1981), so these findings are not unusual or isolated. Such a gap between perception and reality is a problem, especially if, for example, teachers are endeavouring to give equal time and attention to boys and girls. Despite their best intentions, they are probably still favouring boys by allowing them to talk more and, consequently, interacting with them more.

Interruptions are also a feature of conversational dominance. In general, it seems that men interrupt women much more frequently than they interrupt other men and that women tend not to interrupt men. Jennifer Coates (1993) discusses the results of a typical study which showed these results:

> ... men rarely interrupt one another; it is when they are talking to women that they use interruptions. These results indicate that in mixed-sex conversations men infringe women's right to speak, specifically women's right to finish a turn. Conversely, the fact that women used no overlaps [slight over-anticipation of the next speaker's turn] in conversation with men (while they did use some in same-sex conversations) suggests that women are concerned not to violate the man's turn but to wait until he's finished.[74]

It seems too that differences in gender patterns in face-to-face interaction are mirrored in the way women and men behave on the Internet. Susan Herring's discussion of *Gender Differences in Computer-Mediated Communication: Bringing Familiar Baggage to the New Frontier* (1994) suggests that women and men have identifiably different styles on the Internet, despite its apparent democracy and the claim that computer-mediated communication is gender neutral. She found that messages posted by men tended to be longer (i.e., occupied more 'talking time') than those posted by women. Another interesting finding is that:

> A daunting 68 per cent of the messages posted by men made use of an adversarial style in which the poster distanced himself from, criticized, and/or ridiculed other participants, often while promoting his own importance. The few women who participated in the discussion, in contrast, displayed features of attenuation – hedging, apologizing, asking questions rather than making assertions – and a personal orientation, revealing thoughts and feelings and interacting with and supporting others. [75]

COMMUNITY V. CONTEST

Deborah Tannen takes up the issue of how much (or how little) women speak in *You Just Don't Understand: Women and Men in Conversation* (1992), suggesting that we have become accustomed to the fact that men talk more than women and hold the floor, especially in public, and that this expectation is a strong obstacle for women who want to be heard.

> Since more men than women are comfortable holding forth to a crowd, it may well be that it is

difficult for women to get centre stage, regardless of how articulate they are, because a norm is established by which most people expect men and not women to command attention.[76]

Tannen has made a very significant contribution to the whole area of gender differences in communicative styles. *You Just Don't Understand: Women and Men in Conversation* is one of the biggest-selling books ever on a topic related to language. With this book and an earlier one entitled *That's Not What I Meant! How Conversational Style Makes or Breaks Your Relations with Others* (1986), she was very influential in popularising her views on how the styles of men and women differ and how this affects communication between the sexes.

She describes the approaches of women and men to conversation generally as being based on 'community' and 'contest' models:

Women	*Men*
Community	Contest
Rapport talk	Report talk

She proposes that men tend to compete when speaking and to adopt a 'reporting' of information style, displaying knowledge and achievements. By contrast, women attempt to establish links or 'rapport' with others and avoid displaying too much knowledge or boasting about their achievements. Tannen gives examples of one-to-one conversations where the men are holding forth and the women listening:

In all these examples, the men had information to impart and they were imparting it. On the surface, there is nothing surprising or strange about that. What is strange is there are so many situations in which men have factual information to impart to women, and so few in which women have comparable information to impart to men.[77]

There may be a tendency too for women to underplay their intelligence and expertise. There seems to be an unwritten rule that it is unseemly for women to display too much knowledge and that if they do, they are boasting. In my own experience, when I have asked speakers at academic conferences how they would like me to introduce them, I have noticed a marked difference between how PhD students tend to describe how advanced their work is, depending on whether they are women or men. Women are more likely to say 'I'm a PhD student' or 'I'm doing a PhD, whereas men are always 'finishing a PhD', no matter what stage they are at. In fact, many women who were 'doing a PhD' were far more advanced in their work than the men who were supposedly 'finishing' their thesis.

Establishing rapport involves, for example, making sure that everyone is included in the conversation and gets a turn to speak, not dominating others by interrupting them. It also involves politeness strategies, which may translate into 'indirectness', when being polite means not saying exactly what you mean. Women are often accused of being difficult to understand and not saying what they mean.

'Community' strategies are translated into linguistic practice by the following summary of conversational features associated with women:

- Fewer interruptions
- Fewer imperatives
- More questions
- More minimal responses, such as 'yes' and 'mhm'.

In other words, Tannen suggests – and her suggestions are borne out by many other researchers and comment-ators – that women are more inclusive in their interaction when talking to others. They do not monopolise the conversation, rather they ask more questions in order to allow others to participate. They are less likely to disrupt other people's turns by interrupting before other speakers have finished their turn. They indicate that they are listening to what others are saying, and encourage them to continue by saying 'yes' or 'mhm' when appropriate. Rather than giving direct orders such as 'Shut the door!', they ask people to do things politely, as in 'Would you mind shutting the door please?' None of these character-istics is negative. If anything they are highly desirable as ways of avoiding conflict and ensuring smooth inter-personal relations, which would surely collapse if the 'contest' model prevailed. Instead of seeing these features as indications of 'powerless' language, they could be rehabilitated or reclaimed (to use feminist terminology) for the essential social function they perform. In an ideal world, one might expect such a positive contribution to be valued. The reality is, of course, that 'community' strategies are not valued in all environments. While they may be highly regarded when personal relationships need to be built up or mended, they are not as highly regarded in the workplace, where the hierarchical model still operates widely and 'community' strategies such as asking questions or not interrupting may be interpreted as lack of knowledge, conviction, or even leadership qualities.

In another recent book, *Talking from 9 to 5* (1995), Tannen moves beyond the personal conversation to investigate communicative styles in the world of work, looking at how women's style may be contributing to their lack of advancement to top positions. She did this by 'wiring up' hundreds of women and men at work and analysing the recordings to identify possible differences in approach and style. She concludes broadly that women speak more apologetically, men more dominantly. Her work has led to related research on such issues as disputes and arguments at work (as well as at home) and how they are handled differently by women and men. Elizabeth Mapstone's *War of Words: Women and Men Arguing* (1998) makes it clear that many of the old gender stereotypes are alive and well, even in modern business. She claims that women who argue are still likely to be labelled emotional, aggressive or at least disagreeable, while men who argue are considered rational, reasonable and firm. The fact that such views are still widespread, although they may be covert, indicates that not much has changed; we are still a long way from equal treatment.

In business, the use of 'community' type strategies may mean that their users are interpreted as lacking in conviction or unsuited to the tough world of business.

Although it is true that modern views of management strategies stress the importance of teamwork, many workplaces still operate in very hierarchical modes, where you have to be considered tough to get to the top. If women's linguistic strategies are 'community-based' rather than 'contest-based', women may, erroneously, be considered not to be tough enough, on the basis of superficial interpretations of their communicative strategies. If they adopt a more male style, they may be condemned as too loud, too aggressive, too tough or, in a word, 'unladylike'. In an ideal world, people would be able to judge what is, after all, superficial linguistic behaviour, for what it is – superficial. Unfortunately, we have not yet reached that ideal point, and value judgements may be made on the basis of style rather than substance. So, there is a classic double bind for women: however they behave someone will find them lacking.

SAME-SEX CONVERSATIONS

Up until recently, most interest in the dynamics of conversation focused on mixed-sex conversations and the comparisons or contrasts which could be drawn between how women and men behave in conversation with each other. A newer field of enquiry looks at single-sex conversations, particularly those of women in conversation with their friends. An excellent example is *Women Talk: Conversation between Women Friends* (1996) by Jennifer Coates, which describes and analyses a large bank of material gathered from social interaction between close women friends. She states her objectives in writing the book very clearly, underlining the value such talk has for women and contrasting it with how negatively it is viewed by society at large:

> In this book I want to celebrate friendships between women and to affirm the importance of talk for women friends. The talk associated with women is often given derogatory names: gossip, chit-chat, natter. These names demonstrate society's low evaluation of women's cultural practices... Doubtless there are people who will view this book as trivial and unimportant, by association with its subject matter. But we need to challenge the negative social values placed on women's talk and to assert that such talk is culturally significant, and as deserving of attention as any other.[78]

The results of the analysis reveal the complexity and richness of language used by women in conversation among themselves, emphasising the social as well as personal functions of such exchanges. There is obviously still quite a way to go, and many topics of interest to explore, before we understand all the sociolinguistic issues involved fully. Such work may provide a whole new impetus in the area of conversation analysis as well as an understanding of the specificity of function and value of this particular (socially undervalued) category of talk.

CONCLUSION
There are many gender differences in language use in the areas of vocabulary and general approaches to verbal interaction such as conversation. Some of them are

predictable, some are less so. In general, it is true to say that women tend to be (linguistically) more polite than men: they use fewer obscenities, do not interrupt as much, and use conversation as a way of relating to people rather than competing with them. Unfortunately, women's achievements in language, as elsewhere, are undervalued. Despite lip-service being paid to the importance of teamwork and cooperation – the archetypal female style – women's prowess in these areas has not resulted in their being rewarded in the workplace for their abilities and successes. Male style is still considered the norm, the sine qua non of success in business. Most advice (whether in reference to linguistic or general matters) directed at women who want to succeed in a male-dominated world can be summarised by the sentence 'Try to behave in a more masculine way.' Many women have succeeded by doing just that – imitating male styles. Others have adopted a 'celebrating difference' approach, in an attempt to rehabilitate and add value to women's qualities. Whichever approach is adopted by individuals, it is important, at the very least, to be aware of the differences between the styles of women and men and, when making judgements about character, not to confuse superficial linguistic behaviour with personal strengths or weaknesses.

6

'GIRLS' WILL BE WOMEN

'GIRL' TALK

In her book *Language and Woman's Place*, Robin Lakoff pays a lot of attention to the fact that terms for referring to women and men are not parallel, i.e., they are not exact male/female equivalents. The following is a list of supposedly parallel terms:

> man–woman
> gentleman–lady
> boy–girl

Anyone asked to give the masculine or feminine of the above terms would have no difficulty supplying the right answer. On closer inspection, they are not quite as equivalent as they seem. Lakoff refers particularly to the fact that the term 'lady' is replacing 'woman', so that one set of parallel terms has changed to

> man–lady

The reason for this, she suggests, is that 'lady' is being used as a euphemism for 'woman', because of the latter's more sexual connotations. She demonstrates this in the following example:

> She's only twelve but she's already a woman.
> She's only twelve but she's already a lady.[79]

The connotations of the word 'lady' are more 'ladylike' than those of 'woman'. It would be difficult to imagine the 'Women's Liberation Movement' referred to as the 'Ladies Liberation Movement'. Somehow, it does not have quite the same ring to it! In any event, would 'ladies' engage in the same kinds of activities as 'women'? In many clubs and groups, 'ladies' carry out such innocuous activities as making the tea or organising social events using group titles like the 'Ladies Committee'. However, in a delightful example of subversion of the term, Jennifer Coates describes the support network of her friends, whose conversations form the basis of her book *Women Talk*, as 'the Oxton Ladies':

> Over the years, we came to call the group 'the Oxton Ladies' (since we lived in an area of Birkenhead called Oxton) or just 'Ladies', which is ironic, considering that we all loathe the word lady as a term for adult women. The name was initially a joke, parodying those polite but empty all-female Tupperware-style evenings we have all experienced at one time or another. But the name was also a kind of smokescreen to allay the fears of those

(male partners) who feared that we were setting up
a consciousness-raising group. In fact, this was very
much one of the functions of the group . . . [80]

In clubs devoted to sports such as tennis and golf, the
terms used to describe the men's and women's sections
are 'men' and 'ladies'. Any tournament brochures I have
read, in Ireland, have competition sections for 'men' and
'ladies'. In a mixed competition in tennis, one of the rules
is 'each team will consist of two men and two ladies.'
There are 'Men's Doubles, Ladies' Doubles and Mixed
Doubles'. Lakoff suggests that:

organizations of women who have a serious purpose (not merely that of spending time with one
another) cannot use the word 'lady' in their titles,
but less serious ones may.

In the case of tennis and golf clubs, the 'ladies' section
is an addition to the main event, which remains the
'men's' section.[81] Media coverage of sports is often
criticised for the lack of time devoted to women's events,
which usually take second place to men's events. Being
called 'ladies' rather than 'women' does not really make
the reality of these inequalities more palatable.

Another example from the list of supposedly parallel
terms is the pair 'boy–girl'. Women of any age may still
be referred to as 'girls', in phrases like 'the girls in the
office', 'the girls at the desk', even if they are nearing
retirement! As Miller and Swift put it in *The Handbook of
Nonsexist Language* (1981):

Women in full-time jobs may be assistants, clerks, secretaries, executives, book-keepers or managers but, unless their employers are violating the child labour laws, they are rarely girls.[82]

Referring to men as 'boys' beyond the age of maturity is unusual, except for occasional use in phrases like 'a night out with the boys' (when the idea is to enjoy a light-hearted night out). In more serious situations, like the workplace, one does not usually refer to 'the boys in the office' or 'the boys at the desk'. A British insurance company offers 'Car Insurance for Girls', although one would have thought that 'girls' were too young to be driving. It becomes clear from reading the small print in the advertisement that, for this company, the cut-off point for being a 'girl' is twenty-five, since they offer insurance for 'women over twenty-five', under their 'Careful Lady Driver' policy. So, for one insurance company at least, one graduates from being a 'girl' to a 'lady' at the age of twenty-five, and the word 'woman' is reserved strictly for the small print. Needless to say, I have not come across a parallel 'Insurance for Boys'. The very phrase sounds ludicrous and such an aberration would be greeted with hilarity should it ever see the light of day.

On the surface, it may seem flattering for a woman to reach a certain age and still be called a girl. However, on reflection, the connotations of youth and frivolity of the term 'girl' mean that its use is not really an advantage to women, especially not in the workplace, since it reinforces stereotypes about women's roles and capabilities. Are women really being taken seriously if they are being called 'girls'? Probably not. It might have been light-hearted fun for Lorelei Lee to refer to herself as 'a girl like I' in *Gentlemen Prefer Blondes* in the 1950s, but times have changed. Who would ever dare refer to Margaret Thatcher as a 'girl'?

The situation has changed significantly since the 1970s, when the subject of the use of 'girl' and 'lady' was raised, and both sexes have become more sensitised to the negative connotations and associations of the terms. Many women no longer wish to be referred to as 'girls' or 'ladies' and may react negatively if they are addressed in this way.[83] At an academic conference I attended recently, a young woman was taken aback by the fact that a member of the audience wanted to ask a question of 'the lady on the panel'. The questioner – a middle-aged man – intended it as a form of politeness, but it was not perceived as such. It was perceived by the panellist as if he were treating her as a kind of accessory to the 'main' panel, singling her presence out as unusual. The problem is the discrepancy between intention and effect. The result is that confusion may ensue and attempts to be 'polite' may have the opposite effect and lead to misunderstanding. Many women find that being categorised as 'ladies' or 'girls' is limiting, and they would prefer to be called by the appropriate term for adult females, i.e., 'women'.

As a general rule it is not appropriate to refer to adult women as girls, with the possible exception of circumstances where men might be referred to as 'boys' or 'lads'. Equally, it would be more appropriate to use 'ladies' in circumstances when men would be referred to as 'gentlemen'; in other words, the terms should be used in truly parallel ways.

WHEN WOMEN ARE NOT 'LADIES' . . .

As a way of seeing how language represents women and men, it is useful to consider the various terms used to refer to them in dictionaries. There seems to be an imbalance between the number of words with negative and/or sexual connotations that is used to describe women and that used to describe men. (What greater insult is there for a man than to be called 'an old woman'?) In English, there is a series of words including 'tart', 'skirt', 'piece-of-ass', 'slag', 'slut', which have overtly negative sexual connotations. Words describing men in a sexual way are fewer overall and include some which are not really so negative, like 'playboy', 'rake' or 'stud', which may even be considered to be complimentary. Interestingly, there is no female equivalent of 'stud'; a sexually promiscuous woman is a 'nymphomaniac' or worse! Nor is there a male equivalent for 'nymphomaniac' in common usage. The only possible equivalent to 'nymphomania' is 'satyriasis', which is so uncommon that the average speaker of English would probably have difficulty attempting to pronounce it. Looking at *The Shorter Oxford English Dictionary* definitions of the two words gives an interesting perspective on how different the representation of sexual desire is, depending on whether you are describing men or women:

Nymphomania. A feminine disease characterized by morbid and uncontrollable sexual desire.

Satyriasis. Excessively great sexual desire in the male.

Strangely, an excess of sexual desire is categorised as a 'disease' in women but not in men. There is plenty of evidence for the continued existence of a double standard in sexual attitudes.

Languages other than English do not provide any respite from the categorisation of women in negative ways, both in general and sexual terms. A study of general terms describing women is to be found in the standard French dictionary of reference *Le Grand Robert de la Langue Fançaise*, which reveals over 200 words, many of them pejorative, including *'pouffiasse'*, *'putain'*, and *'salope'*.[84] Another prominent commentator on the representation of women in French, Marina Yaguello (1978), comes to the same conclusion, on the basis of finding almost 200 words, many of them pejorative, describing women in a selection of French dictionaries:

> The vast majority of words referring to women are strongly pejorative and carry connotations of hate. Women are fundamentally ugly, both physically and morally, which is at the very least paradoxical in a society which exhorts women to be, above all, beautiful.[85]

Mismatched Pairs

As well as the large number of negative terms to describe women in a variety of modern languages, there are also negative connotations attached to words for women in some apparently parallel pairs. Examples include:

bachelor–spinster
master–mistress
governor–governess

The connotations of a word like 'bachelor' are positive, suggesting a man who is enjoying life as an unmarried man, whereas 'spinster' is overwhelmingly negative, suggesting a woman who has failed to find a husband, as in the pejorative expressions 'left on the shelf' and an 'old maid'. A 'bachelor pad' sounds like a desirable place to be, but there is no such thing as 'a spinster pad', nor would anyone even think of inventing it. The nearest thing to a rehabilitation of the single woman in recent times is the term 'bachelor girl' which was fashionable for a while but seems to have disappeared. There have also been instances of the use of the word 'singleton', meaning 'a single thing as distinct from a pair' (*The Shorter Oxford English Dictionary*) as a gender-neutral term for both sexes, but it has not caught on.

'Master' and 'mistress' show even greater differences in what they denote. 'Master' indicates someone who is in control or who has reached a level of expertise in a particular field. 'Mistress' is also used to refer to someone in control, but it took on a second meaning, one which is now common, that of 'a woman who is involved in a liaison with a married man'. Consequently, the use of 'master' has been extended to include women as in the academic titles 'Master of Arts', 'Master of Laws', and 'Master of Science'. Such are the negative connotations of 'mistress' that no one would want to be called a 'Mistress of Arts'! Another factor in favour of the retention of 'master' is the existence of the verb 'to master', which reinforces the use of the word with the meaning 'to become expert', and there is a whole series of compounds of which 'master' forms part: 'masterpiece, mastermind, mastery, masterful, master class, master plan'.

The differing meanings attached to 'governor' and 'governess' show a similar downgrading of the female version. The word 'governor' evokes images of someone in charge of a large company or institution such as a bank (e.g., the 'Governor of the Bank of England') whereas the word 'governess' brings to mind memories of previous centuries when 'refined' but not wealthy women were responsible for educating children, *à la* Jane Eyre. In other words, the sphere of 'government' in the case of 'governors' is far wider than is the case for 'governesses'. This is another classic example of the male term referring to influence in the public sphere and the female version becoming limited to the private sphere and being seen as very much lower on the social ladder.

These and other examples like 'king/queen' or 'sir/madam' give cause for concern in that they show a consistent downgrading of terms referring to women. It is usual – indeed commonplace – for words to change meaning over time. What is alarming is that such change, in the context of words designating women, should all show the same trend towards a negative redefinition.

Jobs for the 'Girls'

Nowhere in Western society has there been so much consternation about how to deal with the changed status of women than in the workplace. The issue of finding the right way to refer to women who are 'boldly going' into more and more occupations previously dominated by men has been the subject of much debate. Of course the traffic is not all one-way: in an effort to achieve true equality, many more men are being recruited into previously female-dominated occupations, becoming nurses and secretaries and even midwives.[86] In many cases, debate has focused on the terminology to be employed, since equality policies and legislation mean that the substantive issues cannot be challenged. The result is often a reduction of the debate to levels of exceeding pettiness.

Some of the words referring to women's professional occupations are problematic, as they fall into the category discussed in the previous section, where the female version has negative connotations or is a diminutive of the male equivalent. In most cases the masculine form is unmarked and the feminine form is marked by the addition of endings like '-ess', '-ette', '-et', '-enne', '-trix' and '-ine'.[87]

    actor–actress
    author–authoress
    manager–manageress
    mayor–mayoress
    poet–poetess
    priest–priestess
    shepherd–shepherdess
    singer–songstress
    steward–stewardess
    farmer–farmerette
    major–majorette

usher–usherette
star–starlet
comedian–comedienne

These provide further examples of how, in linguistic terms, there is a 'male-as-norm' bias in English and in many other languages (see Chapter 3). It is also true that while the masculine form may be used to refer to all members of a profession ('actor' may be used as a generic term for all actors, whether men or women) the feminine form may not.

In the list above, most of the masculine terms have more seriousness attached to them than the equivalent for women. A chasm separates the activities (and associated esteem) of what is still a linguistic pair: 'major/majorette'! An 'actress' does give an impression of frivolity, whereas an 'actor' does not, so, not surprisingly, many women in the acting profession prefer to be called plain 'actors'. Even the term 'manager' suggests the incumbent has control of a larger enterprise than a 'manageress' has. The term 'farmerette' is a recent invention which shows that titles of occupations for women are still formed by the addition of a diminutive ending. It is sometimes applied to women in agricultural competitions, when it is usually accompanied by a great deal of hilarity. It is difficult to consider the term as anything other than a joke and one can be fairly confident that women in the business of farming would prefer not to be addressed in this way.

It does seem that this kind of differentiation on grounds of gender is dying out, at least to some extent.

The word 'poetess' has not been heard of for some time. The term 'authoress' also seems to be disappearing and its negative connotations are made explicit in the *Collins English Dictionary* definition of the word:

Authoress. Now usually disparaging. A female author.

The gender-neutral term 'writer' is now in common use for authors of both genders. Even 'stewards' and 'stewardesses' have been replaced in the practice of many airlines by 'flight attendants' or 'cabin crew'. It is also true that many women, conscious of the less serious or less important connotations of feminine titles, prefer to be called 'managers' rather than 'manageresses'.

There is an even more obvious problem in the case of professional titles ending with '-man', since the connection between the professional title and a male holder of the title is made explicit in the form of the word, e.g., 'fireman', 'policeman', 'postman', 'salesman', etc. Such terms have been handled in various ways when the post holder is a woman. Intuitively, people feel that sentences like the following are a little odd:

Mary, the postman, arrives about 9 o'clock.
When the policeman asked me where I was going, I told her I was going home.

In practice, many words ending in '-man' have simply been replaced in common usage by '-woman', as in 'postman–postwoman'. This may happen in a purely pragmatic way when it transpires one day that the post is being delivered by a woman. This practical way of dealing with the issue of women fulfilling posts defined in their title by the word 'man' is not entirely satisfactory, although it does at least recognise that women may in fact be carrying out tasks previously done mainly by men. Using '-woman' to replace '-man' in this way is similar to the tendency in some quarters to qualify words which are gender-neutral like 'doctor' or 'lawyer', by adding 'woman', quite unnecessarily, when the doctor or lawyer in question happens to be a woman.

The disadvantage of replacing '-man' with '-woman', or adding 'woman' to a gender-neutral title, is that it focuses on the gender of the person doing the job, rather than on the job itself. The gender of the person doing a particular job is not usually relevant, so there is normally no need to signal it in the job title. Many gender-neutral titles already exist, like 'doctor', 'driver', 'lawyer', 'student', 'teacher', so the idea of gender-neutral titles is not new, nor is it an invention of radical feminists. Others titles have been invented along gender-neutral lines, such as the term 'firefighter', which seems a particularly good innovation, since it provides a genuinely gender-neutral and accurate title. Other examples of terms which perform a similar function are:

foreman–supervisor
watchman–guard

Specifying gender in such circumstances is entirely irrelevant, when it is ability to do the job that is important.

Another way of dealing with the issue of how to alter titles using the word 'man' to describe women holding the relevant post, is to use '-person' as a gender-neutral form, as in 'postperson', and 'chairperson'. This approach represents another attempt by feminists to suggest alternatives to sexist professional titles. While this suggestion is a good idea in theory, in practice things have not always turned out as intended, as may happen when attempts are made to steer language change in a particular direction. 'Chairperson', for example, tends to be used only to refer to women (and not to all people in the chair regardless of gender) and so it has not succeeded in dislodging 'chairman' as the most popular term. The result is that a new pair has been established:

chairman–chairperson

English is, of course, not the only linguistic group which has had to face up to the problem of how to refer to women holders of posts previously occupied predominantly by men. Not all groups have dealt with the issue in the way English has. In many cases different approaches are affected, if not determined, by the type of language in question. The issues are very different in languages which are characterised by grammatical gender, like French, German, Spanish and Italian (see Introduction). In the case of French, for example, the fact that there are two categories of nouns, those which are 'feminine' and those which are 'masculine', means that each noun has to be accompanied by a gender marker: 'le' for masculine, 'la' for 'feminine'. Consequently, gender-neutral forms like 'doctor' or 'teacher', are not possible since a gender marker is obligatory, as in '*le docteur*' and '*le professeur*'. Grammatical gender has caused enormous problems and been an inhibiting factor in attempts to feminise titles in French. Contrary to what has happened in English, where the tendency has been to reduce the amount of differentiation, the tendency in French has been to increase the amount of differentiation by creating a feminine form for every masculine title. Consequently, forms have been created in French which have both a masculine and a feminine form:

teacher:
le professeur (man), *la professeure* (woman)
doctor:
le docteur (man), *la docteure* (woman)

Such forms are used with varying frequency throughout the French-speaking world, with mainland France showing the most reluctance to adopt them.[88]

CONCLUSION

Changes in the status of women have thrown into focus the ways in which women are described by language. Women generally no longer wish to be called 'girls' or even 'ladies'. The days of the 'girls in the office' are numbered, although the message has not yet reached everyone. At a meeting of the hundred most influential women in Ireland, it is reported that the photographer referred to the women present as 'girls' and that this appellation was greeted with howls of protest. It seems that women will no longer be 'girls' – or 'ladies' for that matter.

Another issue highlighted by the change in the status of women is that of occupational titles and how to ensure that they represent women. On the one hand, it is relatively easy to suggest alternatives to be adopted instead of the male titles, but there is no way to control what happens to language in practice. The ultimate fate of any suggestion for linguistic intervention depends firstly on whether or not users actually use it and secondly on how they use it. The pair 'chairman/chairperson' provides an example of the complications involved in attempting to steer language in a particular direction. Intervening in language is fraught with difficulties, since usage and practice – and not intentions – ultimately determine the results.

In the next chapter, we will look at the more general issues surrounding the usage of 'man' and 'he' to refer to all human beings.

7

ONE MAN IN TWO IS A WOMAN

'HE-MAN' LANGUAGE

Much debate has centred around the use of 'man' and 'he' when referring to all human beings. Such uses of 'man' and 'he' are described as generic. The problem with the word 'man' is that it is sometimes used to refer, generically, to all human beings, but at other times it is used to refer to male human beings only. For example, the sentence 'Man is a two-legged animal' refers to all members of the human race, male and female. On the other hand, in the following sentence the word 'man' can only be understood as referring to a male:

> It is a truth universally acknowledged, that a single man in possession of a good fortune, must be in want of a wife. (Jane Austen)

Historically, in English, there was a time when 'man' was a true generic, i.e., it referred to 'a member of the human species', whether male or female, and there were words in Old English which distinguished between an adult male

– 'wer' – and an adult female – 'wif'. Eventually, 'man' was no longer used to refer to individual women but to distinguish an adult male from an adult female.

A similar situation obtained in Latin, where 'homo' designated 'a member of the human species' and there were separate words for man: 'vir' and woman: 'femina'.

homo (human being)
vir (adult male) femina (adult female)

At present, the situation in English is that there are three possible terms to refer to adult human beings:

man (human being)
man (adult male)   woman (adult female)

Some examples of generic use of 'man' and its plural 'men' are:

Time and tide wait for no man.

Every man for himself.

Man is a mammal.

No man is an Island . . . every man is a piece of the Continent (John Donne)

For the apparel oft proclaims the man (Shakespeare)

Man's inhumanity to man

Makes countless thousands mourn! (Burns)

Man is the only animal that blushes. Or needs to. (Mark Twain)

All men are created equal. (American Declaration of Independence)[89]

I may assert Eternal Providence,
And justify the ways of God to men. (Milton)

In most of these cases, it seems pretty obvious that 'man/ men' is generic and consequently that women are at least intended to be included (whatever about social inequalities in the real world!). The same must be true of the use of *'hommes'* (men) in the name of the Paris hotel 'Hotel des Grands Hommes' (literally 'Hotel of Great Men'). It does seem unlikely that the hotel would want to limit its clientele to men![90]

In other cases it is clear that 'man/men' refers to males only. When US President Thomas Jefferson wrote:

No duty the Executive had to perform was so trying
as to put the right man in the right place

the historical context alone is enough for us to conclude that he was using 'man' to mean male human beings, since only men were eligible to occupy certain 'places'. A similar phrase still persists today in expressions like 'the right man for the job', although it is becoming increasingly difficult to maintain and is being replaced by 'the right person for the job', since women are occupying more and more employment positions at different levels. Whether or not this is accompanied by a change in attitude or expectations is a matter of debate to which I will return.

In other cases, the situation is not so clear. When Shakespeare wrote in *Hamlet*:

> What a piece of work is a man! How noble in reason!
> how infinite in faculties! in form and moving, how
> express and admirable! in action, how like an angel!
> in apprehension, how like a god! the beauty of the
> world! the paragon of animals!

did he mean to compliment all human beings, including women? One might assume he did, but some doubt is cast on this assumption by the use of 'a man' (i.e., with an article) rather than 'man' (without an article) which means it is more likely to refer to male persons. The next lines revise the very general terms of the previous lines and leave us in doubt as to the intended meaning:

> And yet, to me, what is this quintessence of dust?
> Man delights not me – no nor woman neither,
> although by your smiling, you seem to say so.

There are many other examples of such ambiguities. Often the use of 'man' or 'men' appears initially to be generic but turns out not to be and actually refers entirely or primarily to men. The difficulty is, of course, the lack of clarity. If it were always possible to know when 'man/men' was referring to all human beings or just to male human beings, there would be no problem.

Liberty means responsibility. That is why most men dread it. (G. B. Shaw)

What is a man,
If his chief good and market of his time
Be but to sleep and feed? a beast, no more.
(Shakespeare)

It is not always possible to conclude satisfactorily which meaning is intended. Samuel Johnson, on being asked whether any man of a modern age could have written *Ossian*, is reported to have replied:

Yes, Sir, many men, many women, and many children.

It appears that Johnson's reply deliberately plays on the ambiguity of interpretation of 'man' in the question put to him, although there was probably no ambiguity intended by the questioner, who probably meant his question to be interpreted as referring to 'male human beings'.

There are many examples of current usage which present similar problems. Philip M. Smith, in his book entitled *Language, the Sexes and Society*, illustrates this ambiguity of usage as follows:

If a woman is swept off a ship into the water, the cry is 'Man overboard!' If she is killed by a hit-and-run driver, the charge is 'manslaughter'! If she is injured on the job, the coverage is 'workman's compensation'! But if she arrives at a threshold marked 'Men Only', she knows the admonition is not intended to bar animals or plants or inanimate objects. It is meant for her.[91]

The result is that it is sometimes difficult to determine which interpretation is intended: all humans or just male humans, and so there are occasions when women must wonder whether they are included or not. This is never the case for men since 'man/men' always, by definition, includes them. Is this an entirely fair burden on approximately 50 per cent of the population – to have to work out whether they are included or not?

Consider for a moment the title of this chapter: 'One Man in Two Is a Woman'. On first reading, you would be forgiven for thinking that it means 50 per cent of male human beings are in reality females, since, in most people's minds, it conjures up images of women walking around masquerading as men. Of course it does not mean that at all; it is in fact simply stating that 50 per cent of the members of the human race are women. The fact that you have to think about what the sentence means, and that it may have two possible interpretations, is ample proof of the confusion which surrounds the usage of the term 'man'. Contrary to some opinions expressed extolling the 'simplicity' of using man as a generic, it is not always so easy to determine which use is intended. One would think that efforts to reduce the ambiguity, for example by replacing generic uses of 'man' with 'person', would be accepted in the interests of clarity. On the contrary, opposition to such change has been strong.

Numerous studies have been done on how 'man' is interpreted. Many people say that there is no problem with the two uses of 'man', and that the context makes it clear which use is meant. This view is not borne out by the many research projects which have been devoted to this issue.[92] A much quoted study[93] was conducted among university students of Sociology, who were asked to select pictures to illustrate essay titles. Those who were given topics such as 'social man', 'economic man' and 'urban man' selected 64 per cent of pictures showing only men, whereas those who were asked to choose pictures to illustrate topics like 'social behaviour' and 'urban behaviour' chose pictures with roughly 50 per cent representation of men and women. This and other studies point to the fact that 'man' is frequently interpreted as sex-specific, i.e., referring to males and could not therefore be considered a true generic. As a consequence, some attempts at generic uses may give rise to humour. Consider the following examples:

Pregnancy in man
A study of the uterus in man.
Man, since he is a mammal, breastfeeds his young.

The first example seems incongruous and evokes images of Arnold Schwarznegger playing the role of a pregnant male in the film *Junior*. The second and third examples are funny since they may be interpreted as suggesting that a male might have a uterus or breastfeed a baby! If 'man' were a true generic, these examples would be interpreted as referring to the species rather than to male members of it and there would be nothing comic, or even remarkable, about them. There is nothing inherently funny in the phrase 'pregnancy in the whale', since 'whale' refers generically to the whole species it designates, in contrast to 'man', which only sometimes refers to all humans.

On occasion the two uses of 'man' appear to be confused, for example, in the sentence:

Primitive man hunted for food for his wife and children.

Other words, such as 'citizen' and 'politician', which supposedly include both women and men, are sometimes found to refer exclusively to men:

A citizen must be allowed to protect his wife and children.
The politicians of France's National Front express some fairly controversial views. Their wives are fairly amazing too.[94]

Such examples are disconcerting, since they appear to suggest that only men – and not women or children – are citizens or even human beings! The two sentences of the last example, taken together, suggest that all of the National Front's politicians are men, since only ' wives' are mentioned and not 'husbands' or 'spouses'. Whatever its anti-feminist leanings, not even the National Front attempts to prohibit women from becoming politicians and it does have elected representatives who are women!

Confusion between the two uses of 'man' seems to throw doubt on the status of women as human beings and gives ample opportunity for putting forward the argument that certain linguistic practices exclude women. It is becoming rare for people to continue to base arguments on the 'inclusiveness' of 'man'. Even *Webster's* Dictionary – and dictionaries are generally conservative rather than radical – suggests that 'man/men' be replaced as generics:

> Although it can well be argued that the word 'man' has historically and traditionally meant 'person' or 'human being' in many contexts, this generic use nevertheless suggests a male image to many readers and listeners. Furthermore, this use of man may not always make clear whether the intended reference is to the male sex or to all human beings. Replace man or men, or words or expressions containing either, when they are clearly intended to refer to a person of either sex or to include members of both sexes.[95]

PRONOUN-ENVY: 'HE'

Just as the noun 'man' is no longer a true generic, the pronoun 'he' and the related form 'his' are problematic . 'He', when used generically, is also supposed to refer to all human beings and so to include women. In grammatical terms, 'he' is a masculine pronoun which replaces or refers back to 'man', whether it means human beings in general or males in particular. It may also be used to replace or refer back to a number of other pronouns or nouns such as 'anybody', 'everybody', 'anyone', 'everyone', 'somebody', 'nobody', 'person', which are sex-indefinite, i.e., not referring specifically to either men or women.

The problems associated with the use of 'he' are rooted in the fact that English does not have a sex-indefinite third-person singular pronoun: for people, the choice is between 'he' or 'she', so it is obligatory to indicate gender. In 1931, A. A. Milne complained of this difficulty in the following terms:

> If the English language had been properly or-ganised . . . then there would be a word which meant both 'he' and 'she', and I could write, 'If John or Mary comes heesh will want to play tennis,' which would save a lot of trouble.[96]

Many agree with him and have lamented this lack in English. His expression of such sentiments proves too that it is not only feminists who bemoan the absence of a sex-indefinite third person singular pronoun. If one existed it might make life easier for a wide range of people.

Interestingly, the situation is different in the third person plural, where 'they' is used for both masculine and feminine. In other words, the plural 'they', (and related forms such as 'their' or 'theirs'[97]) does not specify whether the people being referred to are male or female, but the singular does.

Not all languages have a sex-indefinite third person plural pronoun. In French, for example, there are two third person plural pronouns *'ils/elles'* (masculine and feminine) corresponding to the two third person singular pronouns *'il/elle'*. In the nonsexist language stakes, English can therefore be seen as having an advantage over some other languages, by virtue of having this gender-neutral plural pronoun 'they'.

In the history of attempts to change the use of 'he' as generic, the incident which gave rise to the term 'pronoun envy' stands out. This term – with its obvious Freudian reference – was first used in a letter published by *The Harvard Crimson* journal on 16 November 1971, from seventeen members of the Linguistics Department at Harvard, and was taken up as an article heading by *Newsweek* on 6 December 1971. The letter was a response to a previous letter in the same journal, in which students had called for an end to sexist language in a course they were attending. The Harvard linguists' arguments were based on the assumption that the masculine pronoun was 'neutral':

> For people and pronouns in English the masculine is the unmarked and hence is used as a neutral or unspecified term . . . The fact that the masculine is the unmarked gender in English . . . is simply a feature of grammar. It is unlikely to be an impediment to any change in the patterns of division of labor toward which our society may wish to evolve. There is really no cause for pronoun-envy on the part of those seeking such changes.[98]

Doubt must be cast on the assertion that 'he' really is 'neutral'. In practice, many of the problems discussed earlier in relation to 'man' also occur with 'he' and 'his';

they are supposed to include women but are often interpreted as referring primarily or exclusively to men. Philip M. Smith[99] discusses many studies which conclude that the interpretation of the so-called generic 'he' is not at all as consistent as people might like to think. In two such experiments, students were asked to judge whether pictures of a male or a female could apply to sentences with generic 'he', 'they' or 'he or she'. Surprisingly, 20 per cent of students in the first experiment and 40 per cent in the second decided that the female pictures did not apply to sentences containing generic 'he'. So much for the inclusiveness of 'he'!

As for the masculine being 'simply a feature of grammar', it is useful to consult Ann Bodine's article detailing the history of how 'he' came to be used generically instead of 'he or she' and 'they', which, she suggests, were in common usage before nineteenth-century grammarians took exception to them. Bodine examines the work of an impressive list of grammarians, who, over centuries, proposed the use of 'he' alone as generic. If anything, generic 'he' is an example of an innovation, an attempt to impose a form contrary to usage at the time. Bodine also quotes from an Act of Parliament in 1850 which replaced 'he or she' with 'he' in legislative documents, supposedly for the purpose of concision:

An Act for shortening the language used in Acts of Parliament . . . in all Acts words importing the masculine the masculine gender shall be deemed and taken to include females . . .

There are many such examples of legislative documents declaring that the masculine 'includes' the feminine. In Ireland, The Interpretation Act, 1937, Part III, 11 (b) (and this is repeated in the Interpretation (Amendment) Act, 1993), points out that:

> Every word importing the masculine gender shall, unless the contrary intention appears, be construed as if it also imported the feminine gender;

Interestingly, the previous section dealing with 'singular and plural', states that each 'imports' the other:

> Every word importing the singular shall, unless the contrary intention appears, be construed as if it also imported the plural, and every word importing the plural shall, unless the contrary intention appears, be construed as if it also imported the singular;

In the case of number, there is reciprocity between singular and plural, but not in the case of gender, where clearly the feminine is not intended to 'import' the masculine. To put it in modern terms, the default assumption is that everyone is male unless proven otherwise. The author of a grammar text in the 1960s describes the situation as follows:

> grammatically men are more important than women'.[100]

This seemingly astonishing fact is not only true in the case of English. It is even more apparent to anyone who has learned a modern language like French, which has grammatical gender. One of the grammatical principles affecting French pronouns is that the masculine takes precedence over the feminine. This means that even if a group consists of a hundred women and only one man, the masculine pronoun *'ils'* ('they' masculine) must be used to refer to them. Even though these rules are grammatical, they reflect and reinforce the real-world situation and so one wonders what consequences their repetition might have on those listening to and using them continuously. In my own experience of teaching French, I have found that this rule is so deeply ingrained that students do not even consider whether *'elles'* ('they' feminine) would be appropriate and will translate 'they' as *'ils'* systematically, even when the group is all female and *'ils'* is obviously incorrect!

ANYONE AND EVERYONE

Strict grammarians (often called prescriptive grammarians) insist that 'he' or 'his' are the correct forms to replace words like the sex-indefinite 'anyone', 'everyone', 'nobody', 'somebody', 'person', since they are, technically speaking, singular. Some examples of this use are:

Everyone has his own opinion.

Anyone who wants to ask a question may raise his hand.
Will everyone please take out his book?

Usage in the spoken language, and to some extent in the written language, favours the use of 'their' in these circumstances, although this has been strongly criticised by grammarians for centuries. The problem, as strict grammarians see it, is that 'anyone' and 'everyone' are singular and so should be replaced, when required, by a singular pronoun, i.e., 'he'. It is very easy to find – even in the works of revered authors – examples of 'their' being used as a singular. The following examples are quoted from Jean Aitchison's book *The Language Web*:

> *Eighteenth century*
> If a person is born of a . . . gloomy temper . . . THEY cannot help it.
> *Nineteenth century*
> A person can't help THEIR birth. (William Thackeray)
> But how can you talk with a person if THEY always say the same thing? (Lewis Carroll)
> *Early twentieth century*
> I know when I like a person directly I see THEM. (Virginia Woolf)
> Nobody would ever marry if THEY thought it over. (G. B. Shaw)

In current usage people are more likely to say (1) than (2):
> (1) Will everyone help themselves?
> (2) Will everyone help himself?

In fact, version (1) would be the more likely, certainly in mixed gender groups, and probably even in all-male groups, so established is the singular use of 'they/their' forms. In all-female groups, using (2) would make no sense at all; the people present would probably wonder who was being addressed, since it was obviously not them! It is difficult to imagine, for example, a female teacher in an all-female class asking her pupils: 'Does everyone have his book?'

Logically, it does not appear to make sense to follow the strict grammatical rule, especially when the group being referred to is all-female. Even when the group is not all female some uses of 'he' (or 'his') replacing 'everyone' appear odd and would be unlikely to be found in common usage. Native speakers of English would probably find the following sentence at the limit of acceptability:

When everyone has taken out his book, he will begin to read.

In practice, people use 'they/their' as singular all the time and on many occasions it is the only sensible thing to do. The following example comes from an unidentified *vox populi* commentator on Bill Clinton's political troubles:

Everyone has the right to make their own decision on whether they believe him or not.

There would have been risk of confusion if the sentence had been formulated, in line with the strict grammatical rule on 'everyone' as singular, as follows:

Everyone has the right to make his own decision on
whether he believes him or not.

Using 'they' and 'their' helps to sort out who is being
referred to. The second sentence is not quite so clear,
since there is the difficulty that 'he', 'his' and 'him' do
not all refer to the same person.

Ann Bodine quotes examples from grammar textbooks
which amply demonstrate the difficulty of applying the
rule of referring back to 'everyone' or 'everybody' by using
'he'. For example:

Everyone in the class worried about the midyear
history examination, but they all passed.

In the following sentence no one would find 'he' acceptable:

Everyone in the class worried about the midyear
history examination, but he all passed.

Instead the grammarian suggests that the sentence be
recast in the plural (the same practice as is often adopted
by non-sexist language advocates, for different purposes):

The class members worried about the midyear
history examination, but they all passed.

Such grammatical problems compound the difficulties
with regard to gender. As we have seen, 'he/his' quite
simply do not operate as generics when replacing sex-in-

definite words, since in practice they are often understood as referring to males. Consequently, it is not sensible to continue to consider this usage 'correct', especially in circumstances where it clashes with the real-world situation. A sensible solution to both problems is the acceptance, in line with usage, of 'they' as singular, as has been suggested by nonsexist language reformers.

The history of how 'they/their' came to be criticised is interesting. Deborah Tannen, in her book *Talking from 9 to 5* [101], contends that it was the correct sex-indefinite singular pronoun from at least the year 1500 and that it was as a result of intervention by prescriptive grammarians in the eighteenth and nineteenth centuries that attempts were made to get rid of it and replace it with generic 'he'. In other words, the suggestion that generic 'he' be used is an example of intervention in language, rather than a reflection of usage by speakers of the language. Despite these efforts, 'they/their' as singular have survived. So it is not so much a case of feminists interfering with language by suggesting new ways of expressing things as a case of suggesting that we return to – or rather continue and extend – the way which is long-established. In fact what feminists have recommended is not really revolutionary at all, if anything it privileges what is historically the more traditional way of doing things.

CHANGING 'HE-MAN' LANGUAGE

The very mention of even the possibility of changing language is often greeted with horror or derision. Suggesting that 'chairman' be changed to 'chairperson' regularly causes uproar at meetings, with heated views being expressed on both sides of the argument. Those opposed to change accuse those proposing it of attempting 'to attack or destroy the language'. The subtext (and in some instances the text) goes roughly as follows: How dare people (women?) have the temerity to assault that sacred institution, the English language? Is it not our duty to protect it at all costs from those misguided enough to want to interfere with it? In any case, doesn't 'man' include 'woman', so why all the fuss? The falseness of this last claim has already been established.

There have already been many successful attempts to avoid using 'man', because of the fact that it is not a true generic. A notable example was the naming of a museum located in Hull, in Quebec, which might have been called the Canadian Museum of Man, but was instead called the Canadian Museum of Civilization (or *'Musée Canadien des Civilisations'* in French) following the setting up of a committee to look into the various alternatives. This did not happen without a lot of opposition and public controversy, with letters and articles on the subject occupying a lot of newspaper space in Canada in early 1986[102]. The ultimate success of this enterprise shows that it is not difficult to find alternatives which work (and become part of everyday usage), rather than continue with more traditional terms which can no longer be considered entirely satisfactory.

The real-world situation has obviously had an effect on the use of 'man'. Since more women are occupying more prominent positions in society, some movement can be detected. *Time* magazine, which nominates a 'Man/

Woman of the Year', has announced in its promotional literature that in late 1999 it will be devoting 'an entire issue to the single most influential Person Of The Century'. However, this in itself does not give much cause for rejoicing. The chances that the person chosen will be a woman seem rather remote, if the list of nominees up to 1994 is any indication. From the data given in the *Time* publication *The Face of History: Time Magazine Covers 1923–1994*, I have compiled a list of those selected for the sixty-seven years in which a nomination was given.

'Man' of the Year

Man/Men of the Year	59
Woman/Women of the Year	4
Man/Woman of the Year	1
Couple of the Year	1
Planet of the Year	1
Machine of the Year	1
Total	67

The figures indicate that about 88 per cent of those chosen were, in fact, male. About 6 per cent were female (not too much more than the figure for planets and machines at 3 per cent!). The 'Man/Woman of the Year' 1970 were 'The Middle Americans', the 'Couple of the Year' in 1938, General and Madame Chiang, the 'Planet of the Year' in 1989 was Earth, and the 'Machine of the Year' in 1983 was the Computer. Many comments could be made on the lack of women on the list and on the choice of those women who do appear:

1987   Corazon Aquino
1976   American Women (unnamed)
1953   Queen Elizabeth II
1937   Wallis Warfield Simpson

The absence of women in the annual award category is reflected in a general absence of women from the cover of *Time*. This is confirmed by a study, published in 1989, of *Time* magazine covers which showed that only 14 per cent of covers showed images of women, most of whom were entertainers rather than political leaders.[103]

Despite *Time* magazine's expression of neutrality in using the term 'Person Of The Century', it seems likely that the person chosen will be, in fact, a 'Man of the Century' – ample evidence that linguistic change on its own is not enough; it has to be accompanied by changes in attitude and behaviour. That this is the case is not a reason for not attempting to change language, it means only that language alone cannot change the world; it has to be seen in the wider context of social change.

There are many misconceptions about the nature of linguistic change. Many people seem to view language as an unchanging constant, which must be guarded and protected against those who would destroy it. The reality is that, whether we like it or not, language is always changing and will continue to change. There is no such thing as an unchanging language – it's a contradiction in terms, since language is dynamic. Some elements of language change more quickly than others. Vocabulary is an area where change is rapid: new words appear almost on a daily basis, often without our realising that they have insinuated themselves into our everyday speech. In recent years, computers and communication technology are responsible for introducing a whole host of words into our vocabulary. Can we even remember a time when we did not 'surf the Net' or 'e-mail' our colleagues and friends?

On the other hand, some elements of language change more slowly. Pronouns are a good example of a relatively stable area of language where change is slow. Nevertheless, change does also affect pronouns. English used to have two second person singulars 'thou' and 'thee', both of which have been replaced by 'you', which is now used for both singular and plural. So, it is not only vocabulary which changes; even pronouns, which are part of the 'nuts and bolts' of language, change over time. At any given time, there can be considerable variation among speakers of different varieties of a language. For example, varieties of Irish English (English as spoken in Ireland) still keep the distinction between singular 'you' and plural 'ye', which has disappeared in other varieties of English.[104]

The issue then is not so much whether language should change (it does anyway with or without interference) but who has the right to change it. In many cases, it is hard to avoid the impression that change is resisted because it is being promoted primarily by women. Negative reaction seems to be particularly acute when people (usually, although not always, women) seek to change terms like 'chairman' or, at a more general level, professional titles containing 'man'. What might appear like a very simple change is often fiercely resisted, and arguments based on the 'inclusive' nature of 'man' are trotted out. On the evidence described earlier, it is difficult to imagine that people might still be duped by arguments with such little foundation. Then, of course, the reactions of many people are based on an instinctive response rather than on any objective assessment of the linguistic situation. Even common sense should be enough to convince people that using 'chairperson' rather than 'chairman' is not going to destroy the English language. English has survived far greater threats!

The debate frequently degenerates into sarcasm. Outlandish claims are made to the effect that women want to remove all occurrences of the letters 'm-a-n' from English and replace them with 'person'. The examples used are often ridiculous. No one is suggesting that words like 'mandate', 'manipulate', or 'manuscript' be changed, for the simple reason that the sequence 'man' which they contain, has nothing to do with 'male human being', it comes from the Latin word *'manus'* meaning 'hand'. Arguing on the basis of such examples reduces the debate to an unwarranted level of triviality. The same can be said for the suggestion that women might want to replace 'history' with 'herstory'. Again, the 'his' in 'history' has nothing to do with 'his', referring to a male person, and so the suggestion is little more than a rather silly joke.

It is interesting to examine arguments put forward against forms replacing 'he'. On occasion the complaint is made that using 'he or she' causes pronunciation difficulties. This is hardly true when 'he or she' is said or read out in full. Some find the abbreviated form 's/he', found in written text, problematic: should it be verbalised as 's slash he', 'she or he', or 'he or she'? Since there is more than one possibility it could be construed as slightly more problematic than the full form, but the problem is not an insurmountable one; it does have the advantage of being more economical in the written form and, possibly for this reason, its use has become quite widespread.

Another criticism of 'he or she' is that it is cumbersome, awkward or uneconomical since it involves adding extra words. The advantage of clarity, i.e., being certain that both women and men are included, would seem to outweigh the burden of additional words. Even more importantly, the principle of inclusiveness – and even basic courtesy – would seem to make it well worth the small effort involved. If the principle of economy is held to be the most important, a possible alternative is to use 'she' as a generic, to include males. It is unlikely, however, that those who put forward the principle of economy against the use of 'he or she', would find the principle convincing enough to accept the use of 'she' as an alternative. Some authors use 'she' as a generic, although the practice is not widespread. Deborah Cameron is one such author. In her book *Feminism and Linguistic Theory*[105], she discusses possible opposition to this choice in the following terms:

> If there are any men reading who feel uneasy about being excluded, or not addressed, they may care to consider that many women get this feeling within minutes of opening the vast majority of books, and to reflect on the effect it has.

Using generic 'she' is a radical step, which would probably not find favour in too many quarters. In contrast, using 'he or she' seems rather tame and easy to implement. It also has history on its side, since it is not a new invention, but a return to a previous practice.

Another radical solution is to create a new sex-indefinite singular pronoun, i.e., to use a neologism, instead of trying to adapt or modify the use of existing generics. Many suggestions have been put forward. They include: co, E, ey, hes, hesh, hir, tey, thon. Most of these proposals have not reached the general public and enjoy only very restricted use. Of those mentioned, the best possibility appears to be 'ey'. 'Ey' is one of three forms, 'ey, eir, em', which are quite simply the forms 'they, their, them', with the 'th-' removed, and therefore can be used as singular forms of 'they, their and 'them'. They have the advantages that they are easy to remember and easy to pronounce. Nevertheless, I consider their chances of ever becoming widespread negligible, since people are generally slow to adopt radical solutions.

Another solution to the problem is to avoid the singular, since it is only in the singular that the issue arises. If it is felt that repeating 'he or she' is too heavy, then recasting sentences in the plural, where there is only one form, 'they', is an obvious solution. The same process can be followed to replace 'his' with 'their'.

A doctor is always busy so he may become overworked.
A doctor is always busy so he or she may become overworked.

Doctors are always busy so they may become overworked.

Each student must return his essay next week.
Each student must return his or her essay next week.
Students must return their essays next week.

Among the other possibilities for avoiding generic 'he', the most controversial one, grammatically speaking, is 'they' as singular, since it involves breaking, or at least not observing the grammatical rule of agreement in number. As we saw earlier, in practice, this rule is difficult to observe and may result in nonsensical sentences. It would be very simple, and not at all cumbersome, to go along with usage and accept 'they' as a sex-indefinite singular. If this were accepted as good practice, while there would be a loss in terms of agreement in number, this would be handsomely compensated for by the gain of agreement in gender.

As I mentioned earlier, change in pronouns, although it does happen, is much slower over time than change in vocabulary. It seems as if the pronoun system in English has been modified and 'he' is now used less frequently to refer to all human beings. David Crystal, in *The Cambridge Encyclopedia of Language*, reports on a study which concluded that the use of 'he' (and 'man') forms had fallen dramatically from around 12 per 5000 words to about 4 per 5000 words in a sample of half a million words of American English from 1971 to 1979. Crystal is cautious about the long-term effects, but does stress how unusual such marked change is:

No one knows how long it takes for spoken language to respond to fresh social pressures so that a new usage becomes automatic throughout a community. There are no precedents for the amount of public attention which has been paid to this area of usage, and it is therefore not possible to extrapolate from previous experience of language change. But it is certainly unusual to find a change of such magnitude (affecting an area of grammar, such as the pronoun system) making itself manifest in written language to such an extent within a generation.[106]

CONCLUSION

On the basis of the available evidence it seems clear that there is a linguistic problem with the use of the terms 'man' and 'he', because of the difficulty of distinguishing when they refer to all human beings or to men only. Whatever about the historical situation, it is no longer possible to use 'man' and 'he' in the full knowledge that they will be interpreted as true generics, referring to all human beings. The fact that there is a lack of confidence in their function of representing, when required, both women and men, is sufficient for us to question their continued use as inclusive terms. Generic uses of 'man' and 'he' have decreased significantly, to the point that it is no longer possible to attempt to use them generically without provoking negative comment, not only from feminists. The decrease in the use of 'he' must be regarded as a very significant linguistic achievement since it affects an area of language which is not readily amenable to change.

The next chapter will deal with other nonsexist language issues, those of naming practices and titles.

8

Ms-Titles

What's In A Name?

Names are extremely important to most people. Prospective parents usually spend a long time deciding what names they are going to give their children, and books of names for babies are never far from the best-seller lists. League tables of the most popular names appearing in birth announcements are published in newspapers at the end of each year.[107] The older we get, the lengthier our relationship with our name(s) becomes, and we usually want to keep it that way. People generally do not like it when others get their name wrong – some people feel insulted if others have not taken the trouble to get it right. The irritation factor is even higher when someone repeatedly gets your name wrong. Justin Kaplan and Anne Bernays, in their book, *The Language of Names*, suggest that:

> we feel we must correct someone who has mis-spelled or mispronounced our name . . . because we feel diminished, less lovely, unimportant, not quite visible.[108]

Conversely, people are usually pleased when someone they have previously met remembers their name. We are all human and we like to be noticed. It's not surprising that communications companies training business executives give advice on how to memorise people's names, so that they can make a good – or better – impression on their customers. In the business context, there is a very practical dimension to getting the name right: pleasing the customer and thereby doing business with him or her.

Names, however, are not just a sequence of sounds or letters attributed to individuals; they have enormous symbolic value in society and have great psychological significance for individuals. Philip Smith puts it like this:

> For most of us, a name is much more than just a tag or a label. It is a symbol which stands for the unique combination of characteristics and attributes that defines us as an individual. It is the closest thing that we have to a shorthand for the self-concept.[109]

Viewed from this perspective, the practice of women adopting their husband's name on marriage is a far more significant change than just a minor linguistic adjustment. In fact, the practice of changing one's name on marriage involves not one change but three. The socially correct form of a married woman's name (as exemplified in official invitations and in the social columns of magazines like *Hello* and *OK!*) is considered to be her husband's, with the title changed to 'Mrs', for example, 'Mrs Michael Jones'. Only on losing her husband – through death or divorce – would a woman be expected to style herself 'Mrs Mary Jones'. Of course, if a written invitation is addressed to both husband and wife, the wife is visible only in the 'Mrs' part, since the invitation would read 'Mr and Mrs Michael Jones'. The effect of doing things in this socially prescribed way is that the name of a woman who takes her husband's name on marriage undergoes a change of (1) title, (2) first name and (3) surname; in other words it has a complete makeover, linguistically speaking. In Britain, when Sarah Ferguson married Prince Andrew some years ago, her mother's name – Mrs Hector Barrantes – seemed somewhat incongruous in the context of British royalty. The reason was that Mrs Barrantes – previously Mrs Ferguson – had married an Argentinian and taken his name, following a divorce from her first husband. It was only after her second husband's death that her first name was restored, in line with tradition, and she was referred to as Mrs Susan Barrantes. Where there is a high divorce rate, the chances are that women will go through more than one name change in the course of their lives. In other words they will, to some extent at least, reinvent themselves with each marriage and divorce. This will not be the case for men no matter how many times they marry.

When a woman's name is changed on marriage, it seems clear that there is a serious issue of the woman's identity being completely subsumed under her husband's. This is, of course, at one level, a private matter for individuals and couples to sort out as they see fit. Some women do not seem to mind being called by their husband's name; rather they may see adopting the title of 'Mrs' as an achievement and abandon their birth name without a second thought. However, the story is not really over then, as they will still be asked what their 'maiden name' was, when filling out official documents. The business of changing names has far-reaching influence at various levels of bureaucracy. I have often been asked (along with countless others I assume) to supply not only my own but my mother's 'maiden name' in documents. On enquiring what the relevance of my mother's maiden name was, I have been told it was needed for security reasons or credit clearance. (People usually desist when I tell them my mother died seventeen years ago.) But would it not all be simpler if no one changed their name? Since men do not (usually) change theirs, they are never asked: 'What was your maiden name?' (Does a male equivalent for 'maiden' even exist?) The term 'maiden name' is increasingly being perceived as outdated and is giving way to 'pre-marriage name', even on official documents.[110] Although, theoretically, 'pre-marriage name' is not gender-specific, one wonders whether it would be applied to men. The numbers of men taking their wife's name is on the increase, but the phenomenon is not widespread enough to challenge the status quo.

Twenty-five years ago names were changed almost routinely on marriage, without any questions being raised, but this is no longer the case. Even books on wedding etiquette now tend to include a section on how to handle 'the name problem'. When I got married (in 1980), not changing your name was still a matter for comment in many quarters. Reactions included: 'Doesn't your husband mind?' and 'He must be very tolerant' – a polite way of saying that any man who 'allows' his wife to keep her name must be a wimp! Others enquired: 'Why did you do it?', or 'How did you do it?', to which there is a very simple answer, 'I didn't do anything, I just carried on as before!'. Changing your name involves taking action like visiting the passport office, banks and other institutions to get the necessary paperwork done, whereas not changing your name means you do not have to do any of those things – you just carry on as you were. In purely practical terms, if women marry several times, and keep changing their names, the paperwork must be a nightmare! Another reaction is: 'What's wrong with your husband's name?' This, of course, misses the point completely; the issue is not to do with the aesthetics of either name, it is simply that each belongs to an individual who has been known by this name for some time and neither should be required or expected to change.

Those who are opposed to women keeping their names often raise the objection that since names generally come from the male line, the practice of keeping them is still patriarchal. Although this is a valid point, the main point is, it seems to me, less to do with the origin of the name, than with a person's experience of lifelong familiarity with it. When you have been known by a certain name for maybe twenty or more years, it is part of your identity, bound up with how you see yourself and how the world sees you. Whatever its origin, it is part of you as an individual. It may also be a potent symbol of your place – or the place of your social group – in the world. Could there have been a more powerful political statement than the name Malcolm X, where the X represented the unknown original African name which had been taken away and replaced by a slave name? While the person in the street may not have such strong reasons for making a political statement, the personal significance of names is enormous. When people are deprived of their names and identified by a number, as may happen in cases of incarceration, the effect is to deprive individuals of some of their sense of human dignity.

Surprisingly, many people seem to imagine that the phenomenon of women giving up their names on marriage is nothing more than an administrative convenience[111] and women should be proud and glad to accept their husband's name. This attitude ignores or underestimates the symbolic value of a name, especially to the individual who holds it and is being asked to give it up as if it were an encumbrance, something to be rid of as quickly as possible when one attains the exalted status of 'married woman'. I wonder if the situation were reversed and men were systematically expected to change their names on marriage, while being told that it was 'no big deal', how many of them would accept the situation graciously?

Ms-Appropriate?

Another problem which arises in the context of changing names and on which a lot of attention has been focused, is the question of what the appropriate titles for women are or should be. The invention of 'Ms' has caused widespread controversy. It has been described variously as 'ugly', 'unpronounceable', a 'mongrel construction'[112] and an 'odious little reptile'[113]. And these are some of the milder descriptions! Apart from the controversies relating to 'he' and 'man', 'Ms' is probably the most commented upon aspect of feminist linguistic reform.

In the titles 'Mr' and 'Miss/Mrs', there is an obvious lack of parallelism between those available for men and women. All men (without higher title) are called 'Mr', whereas for women (without higher title) there is a choice between 'Miss' and 'Mrs'. A similar situation exists in French where there is one term for all men, *'Monsieur'*, and two terms for women, *'Mademoiselle'* (unmarried) and *'Madame'* (married), with the important difference that *'Madame'* is often used for unmarried women when they have reached a certain age.[114] Since the difference between 'Miss' and 'Mrs' is 'unmarried' as opposed to 'married', the consequence of using this format for titles is that there is no way of avoiding giving information on women's marital status, whereas no such information is necessary for men. Before the invention of 'Ms', the only way for women to avoid indicating their marital status was by having another title such as 'Doctor', 'Professor', or 'Judge'. Even with one of these titles women are still regularly asked whether they are married or not. It has happened to me on more than one occasion, that on giving my title as 'Doctor', the reply has been: 'Yes, but are you married?', expressed in a rather weary and somewhat impatient tone. Whatever title men give, whether 'Mister' or 'Doctor', it would never be appropriate to reply by putting the question to them: 'Yes, but are you married?' Carol Sarler, in an article in *The Observer* (1 March 1998), describes a similar incident in a police station when a woman reporting a minor traffic accident, giving her title as 'Ms', was reputedly asked: 'Is that Miss or Mrs Ms?'. The habit of receiving information on whether women are married or not seems to be so deeply ingrained socially that even when women hold a title which is not indicative of marital status, or use 'Ms', people may find it disconcerting and just disregard it.

Understandably, many women are not happy with this unnecessary – and often irrelevant – provision of information. Why should it be important at this point in time, whatever about in previous generations, to know a woman's marital status but not a man's? Unless this question is satisfactorily answered, arguments in favour of maintaining the distinction between 'Miss' and 'Mrs' can be based on nothing more than habit or unthinking adherence to tradition.

There are two possible solutions to the problem of lack of parallelism in the titles for men and women. The first is to invent a second term for men so that they too would have two titles, one for single men, one for married, just like women. The US writer and journalist Ambrose Bierce (1842?-1914) ventured a possible title for unmarried men in the course of his article defining 'Miss' in *The Devil's Dictionary* (1906):

Miss, n. A title with which we brand unmarried women to indicate that they are in the market. Miss, Missis (Mrs) and Mister (Mr) are the three most distinctly disagreeable words in the language, in sound and sense. Two are corruptions of Mistress, the other of Master ... If we must have them, let them be consistent and give one to the unmarried man. I venture to suggest Mush, abbreviated to Mh.[115]

Such entertaining expressions of early feminist thought are uncommon – and proof that feminists of the 1970s were not the first to dream up revolutionary ideas about titles! Another interesting point is the fact that titles for both sexes are criticised, as opposed to the usual focus on the problems with women's titles. However, I imagine that suggestions along these lines would not find favour in many quarters. People tend to be anxious to change things when there is a perception of advantage to themselves, and it would be hard to envisage any possible advantage for men in advertising their marital status. More particularly, such a change would involve complicating the system by the addition of a new term, and so the problem is not usually approached in this way.

The second solution is, of course, getting rid of the two titles for women marked for marital status and replacing them with one term, parallel to 'Mr', in other words, the 'Ms' solution. At one level, this solution is attractive as it means simplifying the system. Nonetheless, even twenty-five years after its invention, people are still finding reasons to criticise it. It is probably a tribute to the term's success that it still figures on the agenda of gender issues after such a length of time. One can hardly open a newspaper without finding comments on 'Ms', whether in an article or, very frequently, in the Letters to the Editor section. In the 1970s many people – even feminists – thought it would not catch on. Robin Lakoff did not think much of its chances in 1975:

Until society changes so that the distinction between married and unmarried women is as unimportant in terms of their social position as that between married and unmarried men, the attempt in all probability cannot succeed. Like the attempt to substitute any euphemism for an uncomfortable word, the attempt to do away with Miss and Mrs is doomed to failure if it is not accompanied by a change in society's attitude to what the titles describe.[116]

The issues which Lakoff raises are fundamental ones, i.e., the relationship between language change and change in society. 'Ms' has certainly enjoyed some success; in fact it is often claimed as one of the great successes of the feminist movement, at least in linguistic terms. It is used widely in the written context and regularly appears in guidelines from a wide range of sources, such as publishing houses, governmental organisations and universities. Many organisations have adopted the practice in addressing correspondence and 'Ms' regularly appears as an option on official forms and documents. It is fair to say, however, that its success is limited by the fact that it is frequently used, not as an alternative to 'Miss' and 'Mrs', which was the original intention, but simply as an extra possibility. The result is that many documents now contain, not two, but three possibilities for women, which contrasts conspicuously with a single one for men:

Mr/ Miss/ Mrs/ Ms

When faced with these alternatives, women may wonder what the connotations of the different choices might be.

If they are applying for a job, for example, they may give some thought to how their choice is likely to be interpreted. Those who wish to select 'Ms' may fear that choosing this category may be interpreted as an indication that they are 'ardent feminists'. Conversely, those who select 'Miss' or 'Mrs' may be seen as holding 'traditional' values. In other words, there are even more opportunities for women to give information about themselves, since, whether they like it or not, by the very fact of having to choose, they are also giving information on their attitudes. None of the three choices for women is unmarked or completely neutral, in contrast to the choice 'Mr', which only indicates maleness and nothing more. The most neutral situation is one where there is one term for each gender: 'Ms'/ 'Mr'. Since this format is not used widely, the success of 'Ms' as a replacement for 'Miss' and 'Mrs' must be considered to be qualified.

Ms-Pronunciation?

Whatever people's views on 'Ms', the fact that it has made its appearance in dictionaries means that it has at least reached a level of respectability. Definitions of it appear in the *Collins, Oxford, Chambers* and *Webster's* Dictionaries. *Webster's* even supplies a plural form: 'Mses'. The definitions are all fairly similar as there is general agreement on its substance; the following is the one which appears in the *Webster's Dictionary* (1997):

Ms., a title of respect prefixed to a woman's name: unlike Miss or Mrs., it does not depend upon or indicate her marital status.

What is more controversial is the pronunciation of 'Ms'. For some reason, complaints are frequently voiced to the effect that 'Ms' is 'difficult to pronounce' or even 'un-pronounceable'. There is no linguistic basis for this assertion, although that in itself does not stop people repeating or believing it. This may be because, if someone says something often enough (especially in the media), people seem to think it is a universal truth! The following is a typical example of the kind of argument advanced to support this claim. This example is quoted from an article by Ita O'Kelly-Brown in the *Irish Independent*, of 19 March 1998:

> . . . the reason it is difficult to pronounce is because it doesn't have a vowel in it.

In examining this claim, we need to look at the issue from two perspectives: the written context and the oral context. With regard to the written form of 'Ms', the problem does seem to be that there is no written vowel. If this is thought to be a problem, what about 'Mrs', which does not contain a written vowel either? On that basis, should 'Mrs' also be deemed to be unpronounceable and be banished from English? Somehow those who object to 'Ms' because of the missing vowel do not even seem to notice that 'Mrs' does not have one either! Not only that, but 'Mrs' has a cluster of three consonants, while 'Ms' has two, so if anything, 'Ms' is less complex, having fewer con-sonants, than 'Mrs'. Of course, 'Mr' has no written vowel either and that does not seem to have caused any conster-nation.

In the oral context, there is not really a problem – or at least there should not be. If there is perceived to be one, it is because people base their comments about pronunciation on spelling, which is generally not a good guide to pronunciation, especially in English. The pronunciation of 'Ms' is usually [miz] and this is how it is listed in dictionaries, (with the plural, if listed, being [mizəz]). In other words, a vowel is added to the consonants to form a syllable with the structure: consonant [m]-vowel [i]-consonant [z]. This is an even simpler version of what happens when 'Mrs' is pronounced. 'Mrs' requires two vowels to be added to the written form to give: [misiz]. If anything 'Ms' is easier to pronounce than 'Mrs' and cannot be construed as necessitating complicated articulatory gymnastics – at least not as complicated as those required for 'Mrs'. Another point can be made about the individual sounds which make up the word 'Ms'. It could be described as a selection of the sounds which make up its rivals, 'Miss' and 'Mrs':

'Ms' [miz]
'Miss' [mis]
'Mrs' [misiz]

It is, in that sense, a 'mongrel construction' – although this term is usually used pejoratively – since it is made up of elements already existing in the forms closest to it. In fact, all of the sounds contained in 'Ms' already feature in 'Mrs', another argument for considering it at least as pronounceable as 'Mrs', if not more so, because it is a shorter version. Another factor in its favour is that 'Ms' does not require speakers of English to acquire a new sound or a new combination of sounds, since there are already examples of the sequence [miz] in English, e.g., in the nouns 'mizen', (and as a proper noun in the place name 'Mizen Head') and 'misery'. Consequently, there is nothing new in the pronunciation of 'Ms' and the argument that it is unpronounceable is not sustainable.

CONCLUSION

The issue of titles is a very vexed one. The Women's Movement certainly opened a hornet's nest twenty-five years ago when 'Ms' emerged. The central issue remains that of the representation of women and more particularly the equal representation of women and men. The American tendency to use first names readily has the obvious advantage of avoiding the need for titles. If courtesy titles are to be used it seems only fair that some effort should be made to refer to members of each sex using parallel titles. The bias in using different titles in order to distinguish between married and unmarried women but not men does not seem useful or relevant, especially in the workplace, at the end of the twentieth century. The best solution put forward so far seems to be to use 'Ms' and 'Mr'. Unless and until someone thinks of a better solution, it is the fairest option.

9

Nonsexist Language and Political Correctness

Sexist language

Language has become an important focus of debate on gender issues. There has been much discussion in a variety of social contexts, from academic circles to the media, about particular issues like the use of 'Ms', or more general issues such as gender stereotyping and linguistic inclusiveness. The advent of feminism has led to an increased interest in how gender is encoded in various languages, especially English, although more and more information is being gathered on other languages as the field of language and gender continues its rapid growth.

The existence of linguistic discrimination has been amply demonstrated and the identification of sexist practices in language has led to an increased awareness of how language may not only reflect but perpetuate existing social inequalities. When reference is made in the media to events and organisations like the Conference of Wives of Heads of State and Government of the Americas,[117] it makes one wonder whether it means that only women are allowed into the organisation and the husband of a woman Head of State would not be welcome. Alternatively, is it a warning to any woman who would have the temerity to consider running for such high office that a fundamental qualification for 'Heads of State and Government' is that they must be men, and women need not apply? Of course, the term 'Head of State' is not sexist of itself; what makes it sexist is the assumption, borne out by the use of 'Wives' elsewhere, that it refers exclusively to men. On a more positive note, conferences which used to include programmes for 'wives', now tend to have 'spousal programmes'. With the increase in women's participation in a wider variety of professional categories and political positions, this title is not only gender-neutral, it is also probably a closer representation of reality.

There are many definitions of sexist language. In theory, it refers to any use of language which discriminates on the basis of gender, so sexist language may refer to men as well as women. In practice, many definitions confine themselves to discussing how sexist language refers specifically to women. One such definition is that given by Margaret Doyle in her book *The A-Z of Non-Sexist Language* (1995):

> Sexist language ... refers to terms and usages that exclude or discriminate against women.[118]

The definition supplied by Janet Holmes (1992) is broader and more satisfactory since it allows for inclusion of terms referring to men:

> Sexist language encodes stereotyped attitudes to women and men. In principle, then, the study of sexist language is concerned with the way language expresses both negative and positive stereotypes of both men and women. In practice, research in this area has concentrated on the ways in which language conveys negative attitudes to women.[119]

Although Holmes's definition includes the possibility of positive stereotypes of women being conveyed by language, she recognises the gap between principle and practice. The issue of negative attitudes to women has received most attention and, consequently, sexist language has come to mean, in everyday usage, language which discriminates against women. It is also true to say that the field of language and gender research itself has, in fact, been primarily concerned with women and language, although recently the balance has shifted somewhat and there has been an increase in interest in masculinity and language, both in the media and in academic work. Johnson and Meinhof's (1997) *Language and Masculinity* redresses the balance somewhat by exploring men's linguistic patterns and the creation of male identity through language, looking, for example, at the 'Role of Expletives' and posing questions like: 'Do Men Gossip?'[120]

NONSEXIST LANGUAGE
Since the early 1970s, efforts by feminists to change linguistic practices, by making language more inclusive and eliminating discrimination against women, have

received very mixed reaction. Accusations that women were trying to ruin the English language were – and still are – bandied about, as well as suggestions that women should stop meddling or tampering with language. The arguments put forward against any attempt to change existing practices are interesting from several points of view.[121] They are sometimes contradictory, with the same author suggesting that women should not dream of interfering with something so important as the English language and, almost in the same breath, suggesting that women's linguistic demands are so trivial that they should be disregarded. It is not possible to have it both ways: linguistic issues are either important or trivial, not both at the same time. In any case, if women's demands are trivial, would it not be a simple solution just to give in to them?

The whole issue of nonsexist language can be construed, not surprisingly, as one of power. The key question is who has, or should have, the power to change language? It seems a reasonable deduction that the fact that it is women who are requesting change is enough for it to be resisted. Hill (1986) gives strong expression to this opinion:

Men who criticize women for linguistic innovation frequently use the verb 'meddle' or 'tamper'. Meddling and tampering imply lack of authorization, lack of proper training, lack of justifiable motive. If women 'meddle' with language, the language is bound to suffer. It is one thing for a woman to speak out against injustice; it is quite another for them to presume to alter Mother Tongue![122]

If you compare the positive reception accorded to suggestions about removing negative terms related to race or disability with the negative reaction which suggestions for removing sexist terms receives, there is a very obvious discrepancy of treatment. Who would argue for the retention of words like 'nigger' or 'cripple' on the grounds that they have been around for a long time or because their disappearance would impoverish English? People are usually only too pleased to eliminate such terms because they cause hurt and give offence. Strangely, women are expected to be more thick-skinned and to tolerate being treated as second-class citizens, linguistically speaking. Seemingly minor linguistic adjustments, such as replacing false generics like '-man' words, or 'he' with more gender inclusive or gender neutral terms, or using 'Ms', have caused uproar in some quarters.

The issue of nonsexist language is a very politically charged one with implications going beyond the purely or primarily linguistic. It brings up issues relating to the role of language in society and even the nature of language itself. A very important question is whether or not the language we speak has an influence on or even determines how we see the world. This question is crucial for anyone – not only feminists – who wants to change language or manage it in a particular way. If we do not know, or are unsure of, how language affects society, as well as vice versa, then it is not possible to plan how to intervene in order to steer the process in a particular direction, with any hope of success in achieving the set objective.

The relationship between language and society can be construed in different ways. There are three possible points of view on the issue:

Language creates gender divisions in society
Language reflects gender divisions in society
There is an interplay between language and social
structure[123]

Feminists tend to believe that the language we speak determines how we see the world, and since there is plenty of evidence that language deals unequally with women and men, then language perpetuates a male world view. The logical consequence of this position is that language will have to change radically if gender equality is to be achieved. This is, to some extent, what Mary Daly attempts to do when she creates or recreates language by using titles such as *Gyn/ecology* and *Outercourse* for her books. Another writer who expresses a similar point of view is Dale Spender whose *Man Made Language* is still, after almost twenty years, a source book for many feminist commentators on language. The attractiveness of the standpoint that language determines world view is obvious: it would be convenient if language could be the scapegoat for all sexist evils. The truth of the matter probably lies somewhere in the middle ground: that language plays a role in perpetuating sexism, but that it is just one element in a much larger picture.

Linguists, in general, tend to adopt a more conservative approach to the issue and consider that language reflects the social situation or that there is a reciprocal relationship between language and society. It is obvious that any form of language, however gender-neutral, can be used in sexist ways. For example, I have heard the title 'Ms' being used with stress and intonation patterns which made it sound more like a term of abuse than a nonsexist title. It is true too (as we saw in Chapter 6) that words used to refer to women have tended to acquire negative connotations. So whatever the intention, words may end up with very different uses and connotations from those intended. There is no such thing as a completely neutral language, or one devoid of values (whether negative or positive), however carefully one tries to achieve this objective. So, attempting to change language is a rather complex matter where the results do not necessarily match the intention. A clear example of how usage is the final arbiter of language is the fate of 'chairperson', which was discussed in Chapter 6.

IMPLEMENTING LANGUAGE CHANGE

Proponents of nonsexist language believe that language itself does play a role in, at least, influencing social attitudes (if not determining them). Any attempt at reform presupposes that changing language changes attitudes. Otherwise there would be no point in bothering about it. Everyone would like to know whether linguistic intervention works or not, preferably in advance of undertaking it. If it does not work, many publishers, universities and other institutions could save a lot of time and heart-searching (not to mention money) by leaving things as they are. It is not easy – it may not even be possible – to prove that removing sexism from language affects sexist attitudes significantly. Most advocates of nonsexist language operate from the bottom line that, although it is by no means certain that it will, by itself, effect social change, social change is not going to happen spontaneously, so we may as well take the gamble that it will make a difference. In any case, there seems to be little point in waiting around for society to change first, and hoping that language will somehow magically reflect that change. It might never happen. Standing idly by and doing nothing is hardly an option since there seems to be no shortage of creativity in the case of sexist language. An example is the fact that the meaning of a noun like 'handbag' has been extended to become the verb 'to handbag', with the result that yet another negative image of female behaviour has been created.

Some commentators adopt an optimistic approach to the ultimate success of changing attitudes by making sexist language unacceptable. Deborah Cameron, for example, when commenting on public forms of address in *Verbal Hygiene* (1995), refers to the effect of changing public attitudes on behaviour, drawing a comparison with the change in acceptability which has undoubtedly happened in the case of smoking:

Changing what counts as acceptable public behaviour is one of the ways you go about changing prevailing attitudes – ask anyone who still smokes cigarettes.[124]

It seems that the feminist movement has had some notable successes in implementing linguistic change. It is true that 'Ms' has had considerable success, despite the fact that Robin Lakoff thought (in 1975) that it would not catch on. Notwithstanding its passage into general use as a title and form of address, it has not succeeded in supplanting 'Miss' and 'Mrs', which was the original intention. Use of generic 'he' is on the decline and it has become far more common for people to use alternatives like 'he or she', even if 'she' is sometimes added on seemingly as an afterthought. This change is more significant from a linguistic point of view, since it affects the pronoun system, which is slow to change, in contrast to vocabulary, which tends to change rapidly (See Chapter 7). Ultimately, as in all things to do with language, usage by speakers will be the determining factor.

Guidelines on nonsexist usage have become widespread, and it is standard practice to include recommendations on the subject in style sheets provided by publishing houses for authors. Institutions like universities and various national bodies have also adopted nonsexist linguistic practices and issued guidelines on everything from titles to employment advertisements. An example is the Committee on Equality of Opportunity at University College Cork, (National University of Ireland Cork), which issued its *Non-Sexist Language: A Guide* in 1994. Even the grammar check on my computer, 'Grammatik', exhorts me not to use 'girl' and suggests that I avoid using 'girl' or 'girlish' when referring to adult women, and recommends avoiding 'ladylike' and using instead 'refined, polite, delicate or sensitive'. The publication of *Guidelines for Non-Sexist Usage* by the Linguistic Society of America was an important step for linguists, because linguists usually confine themselves to describing how people actually use language and shrink from pronouncing on how people should use language. The issue, then, has been aired widely.[125]

Focusing on the issues raised by language not only has the effect of raising consciousness about language issues, it helps to draw attention to other issues of gender inequality. Making it less acceptable to use sexist language in public does, at the very least, mean that it is less possible to ignore women and what they have to say. When women make demands for change at this point in time, they are being made against the background of a debate which has been receiving public attention for a long time. When the Co-Presidents of the Green Group in the European Parliament complained (in September 1998) about proposals to name all the buildings of the Parliament in Brussels, Luxembourg and Strasbourg after men, it was possible to see the request in the context of the wider debate on the exclusion of women. While the complaint might have been considered trivial twenty years ago, it is not so easy or politically expedient to minimise or ignore it now.

POLITICAL CORRECTNESS

The attention given to the notion of political correctness has had a noticeable effect on how attempts to implement nonsexist language are perceived. The association of nonsexist language with political correctness has tended to bring the former into disrepute. Strong statements are made to the effect that advocates of language reform are 'policing' language, or even that they are acting as 'thought police'. The recent publication of the *New Oxford Dictionary of English* brought out a rash of accusations that the compilers of the dictionary were giving in to political correctness, especially on the nonsexist language front. A writer in the *Sunday Independent* describes it as a 'sell-out of the English language'.[126] She goes on to complain that the dictionary's acceptance of 'they' as singular (see Chapter 7) proves that

> ideological feminists . . . simply don't know English. They are willing to muddle language in order to satisfy their ideology.

Such displays of pique indicate a lack of knowledge of English and how it works, both at the present time and historically.

Political correctness, although it has been in existence from the 1970s,[127] is now used widely as a tool for criticising a wide range of behaviours and activities. The fact that the term is used primarily by its opponents means that it is generally used pejoratively or ironically. Saying that someone is behaving in a politically-correct manner is invariably a condemnation. It has become a convenient label for criticising nonsexist language, because it situates the debate in a more general context, thus not having the appearance of targeting one particular group. The association of nonsexist language with political correctness has therefore not advanced its cause.

CONCLUSION

It is clear that the process of social change initiated by the feminist movement has brought about a certain amount of linguistic change. Whatever one's position on sexist and nonsexist language, the issues have become impossible to ignore. It is becoming increasingly difficult to remain neutral, since linguistic choices have to be made daily on how to address and refer to women, especially in the workplace. There is no longer a neutral or un-marked choice. For example, when someone uses generic 'he', rather than 'he or she', it indicates a position, situating the user in a 'male as norm' paradigm.

The task for linguists is to continue to investigate how language is used in the construction of meaning and in the management of social relations, how it may play a role in creating or perpetuating certain beliefs and prejudices. Social roles and language are intimately connected in that language is one of the ways in which people, consciously or unconsciously, indicate the social space they occupy. Linguists also need to comment on how linguistic change might take place and to respond objectively to people's genuine fears about 'ruining the language'. There is one thing about which we may be certain: given the central role that language plays in society, it will continue to be a focus of debate – if not a battleground – with strong and sincerely held beliefs being put forward to support or condemn all sides of the argument.

GLOSSARY

Accent refers to pronunciation. Everyone speaks with an accent, related to factors like where they are from, (e.g., a Scottish accent, a Dublin accent), and their socio-economic background, (e.g., an RP accent). (See *Dialect*)

Applied Linguistics is a branch of *Linguistics* concerned with the application of linguistic theories and methodologies to a wide range of related areas. It includes many domains, for example, translation and interpreting, stylistics and computer-assisted language learning. Language teaching and learning are the most widely known and developed areas of interest in Applied Linguistics.

Communicative or Sociolinguistic competence refers to the ability to use language appropriately in all social circumstances. It includes knowledge of politeness strategies, levels of formality and informality. Speakers need communicative/sociolinguistic competence (in addition to linguistic competence) to enable them to interact effectively with other members of their linguistic community.

Community and Contest Models are terms used by the linguist Deborah Tannen to describe gender differences in conversational strategies. In Tannen's view, men adopt a 'contest' or competitive approach, whereas women adopt a more inclusive or 'community' approach, with the emphasis on establishing rapport between speakers.

Conversational Dominance is a term in Discourse Analysis (or more specifically Conversation Analysis) which encompasses several features of conversational strategies, including such subjects as amount of talking time, interruption and topic selection.

Dialect refers to variation at all levels of language: pronunciation, syntax, vocabulary. This is in contrast to *Accent*, which refers to pronunciation only. For linguists, all varieties of a language are dialects of the language and all dialects of a language are equal. The term 'variety' is now more commonly used to refer to this form of variation.

Discourse Analysis analyses samples of language which are larger than the sentence. Discourse analysts study different types of texts, whether written or oral. Examples include conversations (Conversation Analysis), advertisements, news reports, lectures, committee meetings and literary texts.

Glottal stop is a technical phonetic term which describes a consonant articulated by a closure of the vocal chords (situated in the larynx), stopping momentarily the passage of air. It is found in several varieties of English, especially urban accents. An example is when a Cockney speaker pronounces 'bottle', appearing to omit the 't'. The phonetic symbol for a glottal stop is [ʔ].

Language and gender is a sub-field of Sociolinguistics which examines gender differences in language use and differences in how gender is represented by language.

Linguistics is commonly defined as the 'scientific study of language'. This means that linguists attempt to describe comprehensively and objectively how language works. The major fields of research in Linguistics are: phonetics and phonology (sound and sound systems), morphology (word structure), syntax (the sentence), lexicology (vocabulary), semantics (the formal aspects of meaning).

Linguistic competence refers to the ability to use the structures of a language (phonology, morphology, syntax vocabulary) appropriately.

Received Pronunciation (RP) is an accent of British English, not associated with any particular geographical region. Although it is used by only a small percentage of the population of Great Britain, it is the form which is used most frequently for description and for teaching. It is used widely by newsreaders and, consequently, is sometimes referred to as the 'BBC accent'.

Sociolinguistics analyses all aspects of the relationship between language and society, looking especially at variation patterns related to factors such as socio-economic background, race, ethnicity, region, gender and age.

Sociolinguistic variable is a term used by the American linguist William Labov, as part of his variation theory. It refers to any linguistic unit (whether phonological, lexical or syntactical) which varies systematically, in relation to social variables.

Standard refers to the most prestigious variety of a language, as in 'Standard British English', 'Standard Irish English', 'Standard French'. Standard British English may be spoken with different accents, including *RP*. It is the most widely understood, although not the most widely produced, variety of British English.

Variation is the object of study of sociolinguists who examine differences in language related to factors such as socio-economic status, race, ethnicity, region, gender and age.

Variety is now more commonly used (replacing *Dialect*) to refer to variation at all levels of language: pronunciation, syntax, vocabulary.

NOTES

Chapter 1: Bimbos and Battleaxes

1   See for example 'Lawyers and Other Professions' in Des MacHale's *Wit* (1997) Cork: Mercier Press.

2   Quoted from MacHale (1997: 89).

3   Mellor et al. (1984: 1). This book was also published in Australia by Chalkface Press, West Australia. Apparently, high-school English in West Australia devotes major modules to the gender issue.

4   Quoted in an article entitled 'Train Driver Spotting' by Victoria Coren, in *The Guardian*, July 28 1998.

5   United Nations, *The World's Women 1995: Trends and Statistics* (1995) New York, p. xxii.

6   These figures are published in Volume Seven of *Census 96*, as reported in *The Irish Times*, Saturday, 22 August 1998. Of course, while there is a marked increase in rates of participation of women, they continue to be more heavily represented in the non-managerial, non-executive categories.

7   The data quoted are from the Central Statistics Office as reported by *The Sunday Tribune*, 18 October 1998.

8   The preface to the concise edition describes the differences between it and the earlier complete

edition as follows: 'The parent dictionary [Wilson, 1970] is a comprehensive survey of the proverb in Britain, and concentrates particularly on the period up to the seventeenth century, the heyday of the proverb as a vehicle for expressing unquestioned moral truth. It contains proverbs and proverbial phrases both current and obsolete, and illustrates entries only up to the late-nineteenth century. This concise version deals principally with proverbs known in the twentieth century, especially in Britain and America. . . ' (Simpson, 1982: preface).

9   Editors of *New Woman Magazine*, (1993: ix).

10   Editors of *New Woman Magazine*, (1993: 27).

11   Editors of *New Woman Magazine*, (1993: 58).

12   Editors of *New Woman Magazine*, (1993: 8).

13   The first seven proverbs are taken from Wilson (1970). The last four are from Fergusson (1983). As is to be expected, many of the examples quoted in this section appear in both Wilson and Fergusson.

14   These proverbs and their translations are quoted from Laurence Flanagan's *Irish Proverbs* (1995), Dublin: Gill and Macmillan.

15   In Editors of *New Woman Magazine* (1993: 17).

16   Ken Carlton (1998) *Date Talk, Dinner Talk, Pillow Talk*, New York: Avon Books, p. ix.

17   Tannen (1992: 97)

18   Farris, James, 'The Dynamics of Verbal Exchange: a New Foundland Example.', *Current Anthropology*, vol. 4, pp. 307-316, quoted in Maggio, (1988: 55-6).

19   Boyles (1993: 38-9).

Chapter 2: Gender in the Media and Advertising

20   Beasley, Maurine H., 'How Can Media Coverage of Women Be Improved?', in Norris, P. (ed.) (1997) *Women, Media, and Politics,* New York: Oxford University Press, pp. 235-244. The passage in quotation marks is from Douglas, Susan J. (1994) *Where the Girls Are: Growing up Female with the Mass Media,* New York: Times Books, p. 277.

21   Cook (1992: 103).

22   The advertisement appeared in the *Sunday Independent,* 26 July 1998.

23   A photo with this caption appeared in *The Examiner* newspaper, in connection with some equestrian event. I do not know the exact date, but I believe it appeared in Summer 1997.

24   The advertisement I quote from appeared in *The Irish Times* on 26 March 1996 (and probably in numerous other newspapers and on other dates). It was intended to allay customer fears about beef content in babyfood in the wake of the BSE crisis.

25   The figures are taken from data collated by the Office of National Statistics, quoted in an article entitled 'Jobs for the Homeboys', by Jasper Rees in *The Times,* Saturday, 9 May 1998.

26   See *The Irish Times,* Friday, 27 March 1998.

27   As reported by Nicholas Hellen in *The Sunday Times,* 29 March 1998.

28   This (unpublished) study was carried out in 1998 by María José López Arias, a postgraduate student of Applied Linguistics at the National University of Ireland, Cork.

29   Cook, Guy, (1992: 89)

30   This conclusion is reported in *The Sunday Times*, 2 August 1998, in an article by an advertising executive, Trevor Robinson, entitled ' Shockingly Good Adverts for this Crazy World of Ours'. He suggests too that 'In advertising, we are subject to restrictions that would be unthinkable in any other entertainment medium.'

Chapter 3: Variety is the Spice of Language

31   Information on this event is to be found in Robertson, Patrick, *The Shell Book of Firsts* (1986: 178). The first BBC television female announcer was Elizabeth Cowell, 'a doctor's daughter from Cambridge' (a very telling description!). According to Robertson, female candidates for the post of announcer were selected on the basis of their 'tact, personality, a mezzo voice, and attractive features which would appeal equally to both male and female viewers.'

32   Linguists use the term 'accent' to refer to differences in pronunciation only. They use the term 'dialect' to refer to variation in all areas of language - pronunciation, grammar and vocabulary. For a linguist, all forms of a language have equal value; no one form is considered 'better' or more important than any other. To avoid the possible negative connotations of the word 'dialect', linguists more commonly use the term 'variety' to describe the different 'dialects' of a language.

33   See Chapter 4 for discussion of 'Pitch and Intonation'.

34 Examples of such categories in French would be: 'le jour' (the day) and 'la semaine' (the week), with 'le' indicating that the following word is grammatically 'masculine' and 'la' indicating that the following word is grammatically 'feminine'. In languages which have grammatical gender, the categories may not correspond to 'natural gender'. In other words, terms referring to females are not necessarily of 'feminine gender'. An obvious example is the Irish word for 'the girl', 'an cailín', which is 'masculine'.

35 Coates (1993: 49). The source of the table is Pop, S. (1950) *La Dialectologie: Aperçu historique et méthodes d'enquêtes linguistiques*, Université de Louvain.

36 Coates (1993: 51).

37 Coates (1993: 52).

38 In Cameron (1998: 235).

Chapter 4: Gender Differences in Language Use: 'Talking Proper'

39 A shorter version was published in article form in 1973 in *Language and Society*, vol. 2, pp. 45-80.

40 Trudgill (1983b: 96).

41 Linguists and phoneticians (specialists in the sound elements of language) normally use slant lines, / /, or square brackets, [ ], to indicate that they are referring to pronunciation rather than spelling.

42 These examples are quoted widely in Sociolinguistics textbooks. See, for example, Trudgill (1983b: 78-9); Wardhaugh (1992: 314); Holmes (1992: 164-5).

43   Whether or not each of the examples given con-
      stitutes a sociolinguistic variable depends, of
      course, on the variety of English spoken. For
      example, since *r* tends to be pronounced after a
      vowel in all varieties of Irish English, it is not the
      significant variable that it is in English or American
      English. The situation of *t* is also different in Irish
      English. What is being referred to here is the fact
      that *t* may be pronounced as a glottal stop in some
      varieties of English, giving the impression to the
      listener that *t* has disappeared: 'butter' with a glottal
      stop instead of a *t* would sound like 'bu'er', /bʌʔə/.

44   See Wolfram (1969) for this study of Detroit speech
      patterns. The Detroit data are discussed widely by
      sociolinguists. See for example, Trudgill (1983b: 43-
      6, 85) and Holmes (1992: 170).

45   Trudgill (1983b: 91). RP, an abbreviation of
      Received Pronunciation, refers to an accent of
      British English usually favoured by BBC news-
      readers. The two variants which Trudgill is referring
      to are the pronunciation of the vowel in 'ear' as
      either /ɪə/ or /ɛː/, the second variant making 'ear'
      rhyme with 'air'.

46   Trudgill (1983b: 89).

47   Honey (1997: 259).

48   See Holmes (1992: 176-181) for an extended
      analysis of the various issues involved in finding
      explanations for gender differences.

49   Discussion of the learned nature of pitch is also to
      be found in Spender (1990: 38-41).

50   The speech training which Margaret Thatcher

underwent to achieve this very significant change in pitch is described in Atkinson (1984) and quoted in Graddol and Swann (1989: 38).

51   Graddol and Swann (1989: 22).

52   They refer particularly to a study carried out by Sachs, Lieberman and Ericson (1973).

53   Lakoff (1990: 204).

54   King Lear, Act V, Scene iii.

55   Graddol and Swann (1989: 30-1), quoting a study by Henton and Bladon (1985).

56   Cameron (1985: 54).

57   Rising intonation at the end of a declarative is a feature of some regional accents of English. It is particularly associated with New Zealand English and is documented in Allan (1990), who refers to it as HRT (High Rising Terminal). See also Crystal (1995: 249).

58   Lakoff (1975: 17).

59   Lakoff (1975: 15, 16-17). Nowadays, readers are surprised to realise that Lakoff used generic 'he', rather than a gender-inclusive form such as 'he or she'.

60   Dubois, B. L. and Crouch, I. (1975) *Language and Society*, vol. 4, pp. 289-294.

61   Cameron (1985: 56).

62   There are many examples of popularised versions of features of women's speech, which appear regularly in magazines aimed at women. One such example is an article entitled 'Stand Up and Be Counted' published in *U Magazine* in September 1995, in which tag-questions are listed.

63   Trudgill (1983b: 81).

Chapter 5: Gender Differences in Language Use: 'Look Who's Not Talking!'

64   Lakoff (1975: 8-9). In a small-scale study under-
        taken by undergraduates at UCC some years ago,
        the results were, as Lakoff suggests, that the
        women surveyed did have a greater colour
        vocabulary than the men. Colour terms is one of the
        areas of vocabulary which have been most studied
        for gender differences. For further information see
        Frank (1990), Nowaczyk (1982) and Simpson and
        Tarrant (1991).

65   Lakoff (1990: 204).

66   Lakoff (1975: 12).

67   See, for example, Freed and Greenwood (1996) for
        an interesting discussion of the functions of 'you
        know' in conversation. The authors find an almost
        equal distribution of 'you know' among men and
        women (302 to 310) but also find big fluctuations
        in its use by individual speakers regardless of
        gender. They conclude that discourse requirements
        are a more important determining factor than
        gender.

68   These are just some of the examples which might
        be used in formal situations. There are, of course
        numerous informal or slang terms for dying, such
        as 'kicking the bucket', 'snuffing it', 'curtains' etc.

69   A general theory on linguistic politeness strategies
        was developed by Brown and Levinson (1978).

70   This remark is quoted from an article by Jane Taber

in *The Ottawa Citizen*, Saturday, 19 September 1998. My thanks to Margaret Moriarty for bringing the reference to my attention.

71 Lakoff (1990: 149).

72 Gloria Steinem (1983: 180) quoted in Hill (1986: 128).

73 An interesting antidote to this cultural phenomenon is the wedding songs of British Gujurati women analysed by Edwards and Katbamna in Coates and Cameron (1989). (Gujurati is a language of northern India, spoken in this instance by immigrants to Britain.)

74 Coates (1993: 108) discussing a study by Zimmerman and West (1975). Chapter 6 of Coates, from which the quotation is taken, gives a detailed review of other features of communicative competence, including verbosity, hedges, tag-questions, questions, commands and directives, swearing and taboo language, compliments and politeness.

75 Susan Herring is Professor of Linguistics at the University of Texas.

76 Tannen (1992: 136).

77 Tannen (1992:124-5).

78 Coates (1996: 1-2).

Chapter 6: 'Girls' Will Be Women

79 Lakoff (1975: 26)

80 Coates (1996: 3).

81 If anyone is in any doubt about the relative status of women in sports clubs, the debate on the admission of women as full members to these clubs in

Ireland is very enlightening. According to a report in the *Irish Independent*, 1 April 1998, though more women are entitled to become full members, those who do become full members are not necessarily permitted to participate at the same level as men in the decision-making process.

82   Miller and Swift (1980: 68).

83   A letter to *The Irish Times*, on Saturday, 12 September 1998 complained about a sports commentator who referred to members of a camogie team as 'girls' rather than 'women'.

84   See Laubier (1990:108-9) for a full list of words describing women in French.

85   Yaguello (1978:153). 'L'immense majorité des mots qui désignent la femme sont violemment péjoratifs et portent des connotations haineuses. Elle est fondamentalement moche, au physique comme au moral, ce qui est pour le moins paradoxal dans une société qui enjoint aux femmes, avant tout, d'être belles.'

86   An article describing the experience of men who work as midwives in Ireland appeared in *The Irish Times* on 23 November 1998.

87   Some of the feminine endings, such as '-trix' and '-ine', are not very productive, providing very few examples: 'aviator/aviatrix', 'executor/executrix', 'testator/testatrix', 'hero/heroine'.

88   For further discussion of the issue of professional titles in French, see Conrick (1998), 'Linguistic Perspectives on the Feminisation of Professional Titles in Canadian French', *British Journal of Canadian Studies*, vol. 13, no.1. (in press).

Chapter 7: One Man in Two is a Woman

89   *The Declaration of Independence*, 1776, 'We hold these truths to be self-evident, that all men are created equal ... ' For a copy of the text, see *The New Webster's* (1997:1004-5).

90   My thanks to my colleague Dr Grace Neville, who drew my attention to the existence of this hotel. The name presumably derives from the inscription on the Panthéon, which is nearby: 'Aux grands hommes, la patrie reconnaissante ... '

91   Smith (1985: 49)

92   See Martyna (1978) for a summary of studies done on the interpretation of 'man' and 'he'.

93   The study was conducted by Schneider and Hacker (1973) and is quoted in Smith (1985: 50).

94   The 'primitive man' and 'citizen' examples are quoted from a previous publication: Conrick, M., 'Language Gender and Political Correctness', published in Gallagher, Anne (ed.) (1997b) *Living Language*, Language Centre, National University of Ireland, Maynooth, pp. 58-75. The 'politicians' example is quoted from *The Irish Times*, Saturday, 26 September 1998.

95   *The New Webster's* (1997: 975).

96   Stibbs (1992: 144)

97   In grammatical terms, 'they' and 'theirs' are pronouns (as in the sentence 'they know which books are theirs'), whereas 'their' is an adjective ('their books').

98   This controversy is reported by Hill (1986: 50-1).

99   Smith (1985: 52).

100   P. Roberts (1967) *The Roberts English Series*, New York: Harcourt Brace and world, quoted by Bodine (1975: 140).

101   Tannen (1995: 112).

102   See for example the *Toronto Star*, 8 February 1986.

103   The study was by Johnson and Christ (1989). It is quoted in Norris (1997: 151-2).

104   For a discussion of Irish English see Kallen, Jeffrey (ed.) (1997) *Focus on Ireland*, Amsterdam: John Benjamins, Varieties of English around the World Series, vol. 21.

105   Cameron (1985: vii).

106   Crystal (1995: 369). For further discussion, see also Conrick (1997b).

Chapter 8: Ms–Titles

107   In *The Irish Times* list for 1997 (published on 3 January 1998) the three most popular names for girls were: *Sophie, Emily* and *Hannah* and for boys: *Andrew, Patrick* and *Jack*.

108   Kaplan, Justin and Bernays, Anne (1997) *The Language of Names*, New York: Simon and Schuster, p.10.

109   Smith (1985: 38)

110   A recent example of the use of 'pre-marriage name' is to be found in the application form for a certificate of tax-free allowances from the Irish Revenue Commissioners

111   However neat and convenient it may seem to have everyone in a nuclear family called by the same name, it is far from convenient for those trying to trace the female line in a family history, which is rendered extremely difficult by name changes on marriage.

112 Carol Sarler in an article entitled 'Will You Miss Me?', *The Observer*, 1 March 1998 and also Ita O'Kelly-Browne in an article entitled '*Ms*-fits: What's in a Title?', *Irish Independent*, March 19, 1998.

113 Kevin Myers, 'An Irishman's Diary', *The Irish Times*, Friday, October 24 1997.

114 The use of 'Mademoiselle' and 'Madame' does not exactly parallel the use of 'Miss' and 'Mrs'. There has also been debate in France and in other francophone countries about a possible short form of address, along the lines of 'Ms', which would not indicate marital status. One of the suggestions was 'Mad', which is common to both 'Mademoiselle' and 'Madame'.

115 Quoted in Stibbs (1992: 144).

116 Lakoff (1975: 42).

Chapter 9: Nonsexist Language and Political Correctness

117 This event was in the news when it took place in Santiago, Chile, in September 1998, when a lot of attention was focused on Hillary Clinton, who attended.

118 Doyle (1995:1).

119 Holmes (1992:336).

120 'Do Men Gossip? An Analysis of Football Talk on Television' by Sally Johnson and Frank Finlay, (pp. 130-143) gives a fascinating account of a male form of what is stereotypically considered to be a female activity.

121 See Conrick (1997b) for a fuller discussion of arguments against nonsexist usage.

122 Hill (1986:111).

123 See Conrick (forthcoming), Graddol and Swann (1989: 11) and Coates (1993: vi) for further discussion.

124 Cameron (1995:143)

125 See Pauwels (1998) *Women Changing Language* for a full treatment of the history and practice of nonsexist language, which she sees as an example of language planning.

126 The passages quoted are from a newspaper article by Mary Ellen Synon, in the *Sunday Independent*, 16 August 1998.

127 See Cameron (1995) for a description of the history and definition of the term.

REFERENCES AND FURTHER READING

Aitchison, Jean (1997) *The Language Web,* Cambridge: Cambridge University Press.

Atkinson, M. (1984) *Our Masters' Voices: The Language and Body Language of Politics,* London: Methuen.

Allan, Scott (1990) 'The Rise of New Zealand Intonation,' in Bell, A., and Holmes, J., (eds.), *New Zealand Ways of Speaking English,* Clevedon: Multilingual Matters.

Beasley, Maurine H. (1997) 'How Can Media Coverage of Women be Improved?,' in Norris, P. (ed.) *Women, Media, and Politics,* New York: Oxford University Press, pp. 235-244.

Bodine, Ann (1975) 'Androcentrism in Prescriptive Grammar: singular 'they', sex-indefinite 'he', and 'he or she,' in *Language in Society,* vol. 4. no. 2, pp. 129-146.

Boyles, Denis (1993) *The Modern Man's Guide to Modern Women,* New York: HarperCollins.

British Council/ELT [English Language Teacher], *On Balance: Guidelines for the Representation of Women and Men in English Language Teaching Materials,* http://www.britcoun.org/english/eltwom1.htm

Brown, P., and Levinson, S. (1978) 'Universals Of Language Usage: Politeness Phenomena,' in Goody, E. (ed.), *Questions and Politeness: Strategies in Social Interaction*, Cambridge: Cambridge University Press.

Cameron, Deborah (1985) *Feminism and Linguistic Theory*, London: Macmillan.

Cameron, Deborah (1995) *Verbal Hygiene*, London: Routledge.

Cameron, Deborah (ed.) (1998) *The Feminist Critique of Language: A Reader*, London and New York: Routledge.

Carlton, Ken (1998) *Date Talk, Dinner Talk, Pillow Talk*, New York: Avon Books.

Collins English Dictionary (1994) Glasgow: HarperCollins Publishers.

Coates, Jennifer (1993) *Women, Men And Language, A Sociolinguistic Account Of Gender Differences In Language,* London and New York: Longman, second edition, (first edition 1986).

Coates, Jennifer (1996) *Women Talk: Conversation Between Women Friends*, Oxford, UK and Cambridge, Mass., USA: Blackwell.

Coates, Jennifer and Cameron, Deborah (eds.) (1989) *Women in their Speech Communities,* London: Longman.

Conrick, Maeve (1997a) 'Language, Gender and Political Correctness,' in Gallagher, Anne (ed.) *Living Language,* Language Centre, National University of Ireland, Maynooth, pp. 58-75.

Conrick, Maeve (1997b) 'Linguistic Intervention, Prescriptivism and Purism: some issues in the non-sexist language debate', in *Teangeolas, Journal of the Linguistics Institute of Ireland,* no. 36, pp. 22-28.

Conrick, Maeve (1998) 'Linguistic Perspectives on the Feminisation of Professional Titles in Canadian French', *British Journal of Canadian Studies,* vol. 13, no. 1. (in press).

Conrick, Maeve, (forthcoming), 'Linguistics', in Spender, Dale and Kramarae, Cheris (general eds.) *The Routledge International Women's Studies Encyclopedia,* London, New York: Routledge.

Crystal, David (1995) *The Cambridge Encyclopedia of the English Language,* Cambridge: Cambridge University Press.

Doyle, Margaret (1995) *The A-Z of Non-Sexist Language,* London: The Women's Press.

Dunbar, Robin (1996) *Grooming, Gossip and the Evolution of Language,* London: Faber and Faber.

Edelsky, Carole (1981) 'Who's Got the Floor?' *Language in Society,* vol. 10, pp. 383-421.

Editors of New Woman Magazine (1993) *Sounds Like a New Woman,* New York: Penguin Books.

Farris, James (1963) 'The Dynamics of Verbal Exchange: a New Foundland Example.'*Current Anthropology,* vol. 4, pp. 307-316.

Fergusson, Rosalind (1983) *Dictionary of Proverbs,* London: Penguin Books.

Flanagan, Laurence (1995) *Irish Proverbs,* Dublin: Gill and Macmillan.

Frank, Jane (1990) 'Gender Differences in Color Naming: Direct Mail Order Advertisements.' *American Speech*, vol. 65, no. 2, pp. 114-26.

Freed, Alice F., and Greenwood, Alice (1996) 'Women, Men, and Type of Talk: What Makes The Difference?' *Language in Society*, vol. 25, no. 1, pp. 1-26.

Graddol, David, and Swann, Joan (1989) *Gender Voices*, Oxford: Basil Blackwell.

Henton, C. G., and Bladon, A. W. (1985) 'Breathiness in Normal Female Speech: inefficiency versus desirability.' *Language and Communication*, vol. 5, pp. 221-7.

Herring, Susan, (1994) 'Gender Differences in Computer-Mediated Communication: Bringing Familiar Baggage to the New Frontier', URL: http://www.cpsr.org/cpsr/gender/herring.txt

Herring, Susan (1996) *Computer-mediated Communication: linguistic, social and cross-cultural perspectives*, Amsterdam: John Benjamins.

Hill, Alette Olin (1986) *Mother Tongue, Father Time*, Indiana University Press.

Holmes, Janet (1992) *An Introduction to Sociolinguistics*, London and New York: Longman, Learning About Language series.

Honey, John (1997) *Language is Power: The Story of Standard English and its Enemies*, London: Faber and Faber.

Irish National Teachers' Organisation, (1989) *Fair Play for Girls and Boys in Primary Schools*, Dublin: INTO.

Jespersen, Otto (1922) *Language: Its Nature, Development and Origin*, London: Allen and Unwin. Reprinted in Cameron, (1998), pp. 225-241.

Johnson, Sally and Meinhof, Ulrike Hanna (1997) *Language and Masculinity,* Oxford: Blackwell.

Johnson, Sammye and Christ, William G. (1989) 'Women Through "Time": Who Gets Covered,' in *Journalism Quarterly,* no. 65, pp. 889-97.

Kallen, Jeffrey (ed.) (1997) *Focus on Ireland,* Varieties of English Around the World Series, vol. 21, Amsterdam: John Benjamins.

Kaplan Justin, and Bernays, Anne (1997) *The Language of Names,* New York: Simon and Schuster.

Labov, William (1966) *The Social Stratification of English in New York City,* Washington DC: Center for Applied Linguistics.

Labov, William (1972a) *Sociolinguistic Patterns,* Philadelphia: University of Pennsylvania Press.

Labov, William (1972b) *Language in the Inner City: Studies in the Black English Vernacular,* Philadelphia: University of Pennsylvania Press.

Lakoff, Robin (1975) *Language and Woman's Place,* New York: Harper and Row.

Lakoff, Robin Tolmach (1990) *Talking Power: The Politics of Language,* New York: Basic Books (a division of HarperCollins Publishers).

Laubier, Claire (ed.) (1990), *The Condition Of Women In France: 1945 to the Present,* London and New York: Routledge.

Le Grand Robert De La Langue Française (1987) Paris: Editions Le Robert.

LSA Guidelines for Non-Sexist Usage (1992) *Linguistic Society of America Bulletin,* no. 135, pp. 8-9.

MacHale, Des (1997) *Wit,* Cork: Mercier Press

Maggio, Rosalie (1988) *The Nonsexist Word Finder: A Dictionary Of Gender-Free Usage*, Boston: Beacon Press.

Mapstone, Elizabeth (1998) *War of Words: Women and Men Arguing*, Chatto and Windus.

Martyna, Wendy (1978) 'What Does 'He' Mean? Use of the Generic Masculine, *Journal of Communication*, no. 28, pp. 131-138.

Mellor, Bronwyn, with Hemming, Judith, and Leggett, Jane (1984) *Fairy Stories and Folk Tales*, London: ILEA English Centre.

Miller, Casey and Swift, Kate (1981) *The Handbook of Nonsexist Writing, For Writers, Editors and Speakers*, London: The Women's Press.

Milroy, Lesley (1980) *Language and Social Networks*, Oxford: Basil Blackwell.

Norris, Pippa (ed.) (1997) *Women, Media, and Politics*, New York: Oxford University Press.

Nowaczyk, Ronald H. (1982) 'Sex-related Differences in the Color Lexicon', *Language and Speech*, vol. 25, part 3, pp. 257-265.

Pauwels, Anne (1998) *Women Changing Language*, Harlow, Essex: Addison Wesley Longman.

Robertson, Patrick (1986) *The Shell Book of Firsts*, London: Treasure Press.

Sachs, J., Lieberman, P. and Erickson, D. (1973) 'Anatomical and Cultural Determinants of Male and Female Speech.' In Shuy, R.W. and Fasold, R.W. (eds.) *Language Attitudes: Current Trends and Prospects*, Washington: Georgetown University Press, pp. 74-84.

Sadker, Myra and Sadker, David (1985) 'Sexism in the Schoolroom in the '80s', *Psychology Today*, March 1985, pp. 54-57.

Simpson, John (1982) *The Concise Oxford Dictionary of Proverbs*, Oxford: Oxford University Press

Simpson, Jean, and Tarrant, Arthur W.S. (1991) 'Sex- and Age-related Differences in Colour Vocabulary', *Language and Speech*, vol. 34, no. 1, pp. 57-62.

Smith, Philip M. (1985) *Language, the Sexes and Society*, Oxford: Basil Blackwell.

Spender, Dale (1980) *Man Made Language*, London: Routledge and Kegan Paul. (Second edition, (1990), London: Pandora (a Division of Harper Collins).

Steinem, Gloria (1983) *'Men and Women Talking'*, *Outrageous Acts and Everyday Rebellions*, New York: Holt, Rinehart and Winston.

Stibbs, Anne (1992) *Like a Fish Needs a Bicycle*, London: Bloomsbury.

Tannen, Deborah (1986) *That's Not What I Meant! How Conversational Style Makes or Breaks Your Relations with Others*, New York: Ballantine Books.

Tannen, Deborah (1992) *You Just Don't Understand: Women and Men in Conversation*, London: Virago.

Tannen, Deborah (1995) *Talking from 9 to 5*, London: Virago Press.

The Chambers Dictionary (1993) Edinburgh: Chambers Harrap Publishers Ltd.

The New Webster's Encyclopedic Dictionary of the English Language (1997) New York: Gramercy Books (Random House Value Publishing Inc.).

The Shorter Oxford English Dictionary (1973) Oxford:

Oxford University Press, 2 vols.

Trudgill, Peter (1974) *The Social Differentiation of English in Norwich*, Cambridge: Cambridge University Press.

Trudgill, Peter, (1983a), *On Dialect, Social and Geographical Perspectives*, Oxford: Blackwell.

Trudgill, Peter (1983b) *Sociolinguistics: An Introduction to Language and Society*, Harmondsworth: Penguin (first edition 1974).

Time Magazine (1995) *The Face of History: Time Magazine Covers 1923–994*, U.S.A.

University College Cork, Committee on Equality of Opportunity (1994) *Non-Sexist Language: A Guide.*

Wardhaugh, Ronald (1992) *An Introduction to Sociolinguistics*, Oxford and Cambridge, Mass.: Blackwell, (second edition), (first edition 1986).

Wilson, F. P. (ed.) (1970) *The Oxford Dictionary of English Proverbs*, Oxford: Oxford University Press.

Wolfram, Walter A. (1969) *A Sociolinguistic Description of Detroit Negro Speech*, Washington DC: Center for Applied Linguistics.

Yaguello, Marina (1978) *Les Mots et Les Femmes*, Paris: Payot.

Yaguello, Marina (1998) *Petits Faits de Langue*, Paris: Editions du Seuil.

Zimmerman, Don and West, Candace (1975) 'Sex Roles, Interruptions and Silences in Conversation', in Thorne, Barrie and Henley, Nancy (eds.) *Language and Sex: Difference and Dominance*, Rowley, Mass.: Newbury House.